GHETTO
SCHOOL

GHETTO SCHOOL

CLASS WARFARE IN AN ELEMENTARY SCHOOL

Gerald Levy

PEGASUS   *NEW YORK*

ACKNOWLEDGMENTS

IN ALL STAGES of this project and the preliminary problems leading up to it, I owe a debt of gratitude to Arthur Vidich for his ideas, his technical assistance, and his personal support. I am grateful for the indispensible editorial advice of David Pursglove. Key chapters on the teachers are heavily dependent on the work of Joseph Bensman, particularly his work on the "administrative liberal." I must also acknowledge my dependence on the work of Irving Goffman. Of those authors whose work on education is well known, I am particularly indebted to Paul Goodman, Kenneth Clark, Jonathan Kozol, and Herbert Kohl. At all stages of the project I was thankful for the personal support and helpful criticism of Nick Alex, David Harvey, and Laurin Raiken. At various points friends and colleagues were kind enough to read and comment on the manuscript. They are: Peter Mechanick, Charles McReynolds, Victor Gioscia, Karen Gaylord, Rose Brandzell, Deborah Offenbacher, Emil Oestereicher, Robert Bookstein, Henry Etzkowitz, Norman Matlin, and Barry Levine. I conducted the field work and wrote much of the study while attending the Graduate Faculty of the New School for Social Research. It is unfortunate that the one teacher at Midway who knew of my work must remain nameless. He provided me with crucial information about the school and commented on an earlier draft of this book. Thanks are due to Toni Hess and Barbara Weinstein for the thankless job of typing the manuscript. Thanks to Jan Goldstein and all the people at Pegasus for their enthusiasm for the study. Finally thanks to my wife, Harriett who assisted in the typing and in innumerable other ways.

Gerald Levy
New York, 1969

CONTENTS

PREFACE

Theoretical Note

LOCATED between American society and its lower classes are a variety of welfare institutions. Schools, hospitals, welfare centers, nursing homes, social work agencies, prisons, and recent "War on Poverty" programs service lower-class minorities, poor, "criminal," elderly, and infirm. As official avenues of social and economic redress, these locally administered agencies provide the pivotal point of contact between American society and its lower classes, define the terms upon which lower-class individuals can make claims on American society, and set the limits of the claims. Through its welfare institutions American society communicates to and maintains distance from its lower classes.

In Black and Puerto Rican ghettos, welfare institutions assume peculiar significance. For many ghetto families contact with white society is exclusively limited to commuting social workers, teachers, doctors, nurses, cops, ghetto businessmen, and landlords. Ghetto inhabitants are ever aware of the presence of these commuters and the dominance of the institutions they represent. For many the presence and dominance approaches the quality of a southern plantation or a company town.

With the possible exception of police agencies, welfare

institutions view themselves as agents of social amelioration. Welfare functionaries would like to think of themselves as liberal humanitarians working in the interest of the poor and "culturally deprived." In adopting this image of their work they attempt to distinguish themselves from greedy business-men, corrupt politicians, advertising executives, and uncommitted intellectuals, all of whom lack the social conscience, human sensitivity, political independence, and moral integrity crucial to the ameliorative task.

Likewise, the liberal middle and upper classes view the welfare institutions as extensions of their liberality and concrete examples of historical progress. Distant from the lower-class objects of sympathy and the agencies through which the sympathy is expressed, the liberal higher classes delegate to welfare institutions the responsibility for the solution of domestic problems by proxy. In looking to the welfare institutions for the fruition of their political ideology, they are essentially correct. For the empirical application of welfare liberalism is located within contemporary schools, hospitals, and welfare centers.

But America's communication with its lower classes takes place within a political context which transcends the intentions of its welfare liberals. For American society is unwilling or unable to ameliorate its lower classes on their terms or even on the terms of its liberal higher classes. The lower classes are poignantly aware of the limits of ameliorative redress and the gap between the liberal rhetoric and the administrative reality. They use the imagery of humanitarian liberalism as a comparative device to express their dissatisfaction with welfare institutions and to attack the integrity of the welfare employees. To their chagrin sensitive psychiatrists, idealistic social workers, and dedicated teachers are often lumped with the very businessmen, politicians, and policemen from whom they wish to be distinguished.

However, welfare liberals cannot afford to view their institutions from the perspective of the lower classes. For doing so would entail not only a condemnation of a political process they support and participate in, but a deflation of their sense of moral superiority over conservatives. Thus they attribute the failure of welfare institutions to accomplish its goals to budgetary insufficiencies and administrative ineffectiveness. Their analysis focuses on corrections that have to be made in the welfare system rather than on the political tasks of welfare administration.

By concentrating on the failures of the illusory ameliorative process it would like to see occurring, the liberal critique avoids coming to terms with the actual process, the tasks that are completed, and the logical relationship of the process to larger political reality. Since welfare institutions are crucial in working out domestic policy toward the lower classes, it is important that they be described according to the political tasks they perform.*

The ghetto school is a poignant illustration. American society defines its ghetto schools as the vehicle of lower-class Black mobility. On schools is placed the burden of preparing ghetto youth for middle-class life. But those who believe in the public goals of ghetto education assume that society is prepared to absorb its lower classes. When ghetto education fails to accomplish its public goals these same people blame the inadequacy of the education if they are liberals and the inferiority of the children if they are conservative. Few educational ideologists focus on the political task of ghetto schools.

---

*Within the welfare institutions, broad domestic policy toward the lower classes is implemented in the same way military and governmental bureaucracies implement foreign policy. In this sense the welfare bureaucracies are fundamentally political. There are two distinct aspects of politics: the making of policy and the implementation of policy. This study of Midway School assumes that a societal policy exists which may have a rationality independent of the intentions of policy makers and implementors at all levels. But our concern here is not with the making of policy but with its implementation at the local level.

Ghetto children's major direct experience with American society takes place in school. From the age of five through sixteen they are in school six hours a day, five days a week. Through this long-term residency the ghetto child learns the terms of success and failure in a society that does not favor him. The description of what *is* learned aside from what is not learned is crucial to an understanding of ghetto education.

Ghetto teachers and administrators are the carriers of a political process on the direct and personal level. As agents of the larger society they transmit what American society communicates to its ghetto children. Regardless of their intentions, they participate in a political process over which they have little control. It is important here to describe the political process, how they are initiated into the process, and how they mediate the discrepancy between their image of education and the educational tasks they see themselves performing.

Thus Midway School, as a case study of a welfare institution and its relationship to lower-class youth, is approached from the perspective of the logic of its education and the political task it assumes independently of the intentions of its participants.

Methodological Note

In September, 1967, I accepted a teaching assignment in Midway School for the express purpose of doing a study. With the exception of one teacher who shared my biases, I at no time informed anyone at Midway that I was studying him.

As a "floater" teacher I was not given responsibility for any one class but took over classes of absent teachers, gave regular teachers their "preps,"* and observed and assisted regular

*A free period granted for the purpose of preparing lessons.

teachers in their classes. In this way I was able to observe all of Midway's teachers and most of the children in the classrooms. Whenever possible I attended staff meetings, P.T.A. meetings, training conferences, teacher bull-sessions in the lunchroom, and children's bull-sessions in the halls, the playground, and the classroom. For a year I observed and participated in the daily life of the school. I also had extended conversations with teachers, administrators, parents, and children. In the early months of my stay I took the part of an enthusiastic novice anxious to learn how to be a teacher and curious about Midway's past. This approach was especially fruitful with Midway's veteran teachers who seemed to thrive on this interest in their careers.

In gaining entrance to Midway's life as a teacher, I could not avoid becoming a part of the social process I was observing. As I found myself implicated in a process of which I was critical, I attempted, like many of Midway's teachers, to rationalize my participation by assuring myself that my involvement was less implicating than that of other teachers. Ultimately I attempted to justify my participation on the grounds that I was doing a study. Being an observer does not absolve me from responsibility as a participant. So in attempting a description and analysis of Midway, I cannot separate myself from the object of description or exempt myself from any critical interpretations that the reader may apply to the school.

MIDWAY SCHOOL is located between a Black ghetto and a Puerto Rican ghetto. The first thing one notices about the school is that it stands out. Its straight modern lines and almost bright orange brick contrast sharply with the rest of the neighborhood. Although the school was built in 1954, its three floors still look new, perhaps because the surrounding community appears so dilapidated. To the stranger the school appears as an outpost of civilization and progress.

Beginning teachers are visibly relieved when they first approach the school. It is more like those schools they attended as children and not at all like the "ghetto schools" they have read about and seen in movies. Since the district office, from which beginning teachers are assigned to other schools in the district, is located within sight of Midway, teachers choose Midway when given a choice: at least Midway appears to be clean and new. But there is a deeper dimension to their initial image of the school. Most of the teachers are assigned to District 7 against their will and they harbor the vague hope that this clean, modern school will protect them from the ghetto.

If the first impression of Midway contradicts the expectations of new teachers, the surrounding neighborhood does not. The streets and sidewalks in Midway's immediate vicinity are

often cluttered with litter and garbage. Five-story tenements
are flanked by shabby houses and wooden shacks, many
broken down and abandoned. On Bickford Avenue, adjoining
the school, are grocery stores, liquor stores, beauty parlors,
barber shops, Puerto Rican restaurants, a candy store, and a
Jewish law office. Half of the stores on Bickford Avenue are
currently vacant. Young men hang around the street corner
with the older men and stare at the white teachers as they
walk into the school. Cops and hungry-looking dogs patrol
the street.

But there are other varieties of life outside the school that
the stranger would not immediately view as repulsive. On
Bickford Avenue Puerto Rican families migrate between their
upstairs apartments and their grocery stores and restaurants.
People laugh and shout out of windows to their relatives and
friends in the street. Old men loaf on the street, play dominoes,
and drink beer. Children play in the park adjoining the school
and run free in the street. The stranger senses a certain vitality
in the neighborhood which he finds congenial as long as it
does not occur in the school.

Entering Midway, the stranger is further impressed with the
school's sleek and modern interior. Just inside the main entrance stands a spacious gym and aseptic lunchroom with
white-uniformed dietitians and kitchen help. Across the hall
is a 500-seat auditorium, each side of which is lined with
framed prints by Renoir, Rembrandt, and Picasso, donated
by the P.T.A. Long, well-lighted hallways have white lines on
each side for the children to march on. Glass-encased cabinets
in front of the main office display kindergarten children's clay
sculptures, their latest paintings, their toy drums and flutes
with neatly lettered captions overhead, THE JOY OF MUSIC
and WE EXPRESS OURSELVES THROUGH ART. Farther down the
hall a third-grade bulletin board displays neatly written compositions, each with a red star, a "very good," and a large
lettered sign, WE ARE BURSTING WITH PRIDE.

Before the teachers and children arrive, the main office is already bustling with secretaries taking calls from teachers "calling in sick." Walking past the office and peering through the windows of the classroom doors, the stranger notices clean-wiped blackboards, well-swept floors, straight rows of desks, plants in the windows, charts, maps, posters of foreign countries, and pictures of presidents, governors, mayors, and Black leaders on the walls. Most classrooms have library corners, and all display the American flag. Many classes have seasonal decorations and almost all display children's compositions, "perfect" spelling tests, "100%" arithmetic tests, and "current events" newspaper articles on the bulletin boards. Every fifth or sixth classroom has a "special commendation" from Mr. Dobson (the principal) taped on the door.

Midway's spotless halls, modern eating and recreational facilities, "educational" decorations, and well-ordered, cheery classrooms are enhanced by its two new wings which jut out west of the old main building along Bickford Avenue and create a little playground, with newly planted trees and shrubbery, between them. Shining hallways and bright but not overbearing pastel colors, unscratched floors, and unmarked desks lend an air of comfort and gaiety to the school. Incorporated into the new wings are all the latest educational equipment and innovations. Some classrooms have dividers so that two small classrooms can be combined into one for a lesson from a visiting specialist or two classes can undertake "joint projects" together. There is a special art room situated to take advantage of the sun with large basins for cleaning art materials and an adjoining supply room loaded with supplies. Several small rooms marked "junior guidance" have been set aside for the time when special guidance teachers will be provided for in the budget. Then "disruptive" children will be removed from their regular classes and placed in a guidance class until they have learned to "adjust" to the classroom. Until guidance classes are budgeted, the rooms are used by research psychologists from the Board of Education and a local university who conduct educational experiments on the children. Other small rooms adjoining regular classrooms have one-way see-through windows so that classes can be observed by other teachers, supervisors, officials from the Board of Education, student teachers, and researchers without the children, or even the teacher, knowing it.

Midway's five supply rooms are generously stocked with all the latest science equipment, tape recorders, phonographs, movie and slide projectors, records, and numerous other "audio-visual aids." A guidance counselor and her intern, a lower-grade reading coordinator, a reading specialist, a teacher training coordinator, a part-time psychologist, and a part-time speech therapist, each with his own office, offer "special services" to the children and "inexperienced" teachers. A library stocked with children's books for all relevant ages covering all relevant fields with a full-time librarian and two "paraprofessional" assistants takes up the space of three classrooms in the new wing. Touring the first floor and inspecting its many classrooms, stockrooms, specialist offices, and eating and recreational facilities, the hopeful stranger might conclude that here is a place where these unfortunate children are provided for. For him, after a first glance at Midway, without its teachers and children, the school takes on the quality of an oasis in which the children can get the nourishment that life in the ghetto deprives them of.

Midway goes to great extremes to sustain its image of modernity, cleanliness, and progress. Local residents of Randolph Park, hired as janitors and maids, daily sweep and often mop the halls and classroom floors, clean the blackboards, and line up the desks if the residing class has not. Midway's fourteen bathrooms are given a thorough cleaning daily as is the new lunchroom and its modern kitchen, and the teachers' lunchroom. The offices of the principal, the two assistant principals, and various specialists and coordinators are also cleaned and dusted daily. Broken windows are replaced, damaged classroom equipment is fixed, blown lights are replaced, and broken toilets are repaired as quickly as possible. Anything within the realm of technical or budgetary possibility is done to maintain the contrast between the "broken-down" "disorganized" neighborhood and the school.

On closer inspection of the second and third floors, however, the stranger discovers that the contrast is less perfectly maintained than his first impression would allow. Already in some classes in the new wing, desks are beginning to show the scratches and carvings characteristic of older desks. Some rooms show paint markings and accumulated food and ink stains that the janitors have given up trying to wash away. A few of the third-floor hall bulletin-board displays have been ripped down and replaced by pornographic markings and phrases alluding to certain teachers and administrators. In many upper-floor classrooms broken windows remain unreplaced, sharpeners don't sharpen, pointers hang broken, marks remain on the walls. Much of the highly valued science equipment and audio-visual aids remain crated and unused. The newly planted shrubbery alongside the new wings has been stepped on and broken, the protective chain surrounding them ignored. The conscientious attempts of the janitorial staff to preserve the school's image cannot keep up with the high rate of breakdown, sabotage, and destruction.

About 8:15 A.M. Midway's teachers and children begin to arrive. The teachers wade their way through scores of children waiting to get into the auditorium, and make their way to the main office to punch in, check their mail, and pick up their keys. Floater teachers (those who don't have a regular class) check the bulletin board to see if they have been assigned to a class whose regular teacher has called in sick. If not given a class they smile and make their way to Miss Ryley's office in Room 113 to pick up their program. Otherwise they grumble almost inaudibly and pick up their keys. A secretary loudly reminds an inexperienced teacher to get his attendance reports in on time. A parent waits outside Mr. Dobson's office and stares angrily at the teachers.

Back at the main entrance the children are now filing into the auditorium. Some sit down, talk softly to each other, and chew on candy and bubble gum. Others run around the aisles, pick fights with other children, run up on the stage. Others try to break through the line of junior guards which blocks the hall beyond the auditorium. A few make it through and run around the halls. As more children and more teachers arrive the auditorium gets noisier until Mr. Morton (assistant principal) blows his whistle and screams into the microphone "By now everyone should be sitting in their seats and facing front." Another teacher screams to her class "You're still not quiet." Morton continues "Face front—Okay, that girl in the white sweater, if you're not quiet we can stay here until six o'clock." As the assembly quiets down, Morton calls the classes that are quietest and, led by their teacher, they file out of the auditorium, two by two. Occasionally on the way to their classrooms, marching classes break formation and run around the hall until they are herded back into line by an irate, screaming teacher or assistant principal.

Inside the classrooms everything is supposed to be organized. The children sit still and do their work if the classroom is under control. But often the classes are more like the uncontrolled auditorium and the street. Children can often be seen running around the classroom, talking, yelling, laughing, fighting, dancing, singing, and eating.

Back in the office the angry parent leaves Dobson's office accompanied by Mrs. Talbot, the guidance counselor. They head for her office across the hall for a conference. Three "disruptive" children who have been sent to the office by their teachers sit on the bench next to the mail box, occasionally chatting with the secretaries or the late-arriving teachers. Later in the day a child is sent to the office crying uncontrollably.

When the secretaries are unable to get him to stop, Dobson and Morton, who are conversing in the principal's office, are called over. When the child continues crying after they arrive Dobson blurts out, "This is disgusting behavior, Robert. If you do not stop, I will have to call your father, and he will have to come all the way from work and will have to take you home."

During the third period there is a jazz concert in the auditorium for the upper-grade children. The children sway to the beat of the music, snapping their fingers, and doing little dance steps in their seats. The teachers stand behind their classes, exaggeratedly straight. As the children become more expressive, the teachers stiffen more, their eyes darting about. If a child sways too far, or taps his feet, gyrates his body too uninhibitedly or snaps his fingers too loudly, a teacher quickly walks over and silences him. At one point the movement of the children approaches a breakdown in control. A Black teacher, Mr. Johnson, stops the music and warns the children that they better behave themselves or they will be sent back to their classes.

As the day progresses, teachers on their free periods drop into the office to pick up form letters to be sent to the parents, go to the teachers' lunchroom for a quick doze or to read the newspaper, the washroom for a smoke, or sneak out to the corner store for a snack. During the lunch hour, the lunchroom is filled with teachers gossiping about their troubles with administrators, children, and parents. Mrs. Jackson, president of the P.T.A., has been walking the halls and checking up on teachers. She was in Dobson's office for an hour this morning and it is rumored that Stratton, the district superintendent, will be walking the halls this afternoon.

Downstairs in the children's lunchroom, several teachers, a few community aides, and five or six volunteer parents chase children around the lunchroom. Junior guards patrol the halls in vain, grabbing at children who have broken through the lines. Mrs. Jackson, returned from her tour of the halls, stops by the lunchroom, gives a group of passing teachers on their way to the nearby Jewish delicatessen a dirty look, and peers in at the noisy children through the lunchroom windows. In a voice where everyone nearby can hear her, she says to herself, "This is disgraceful." The group of teachers keeps on walking.

Later in the afternoon, the halls are filled with children expelled and escaped from their classes, who, joined by children from Porter Junior High School across the park, run around the halls, disturb the classes, and evade roving administrators and volunteer parents patroling the halls.

Almost daily, officials from the Board of Education are given guided tours of the new wing by Stratton who offers Midway as an example of innovative education. Representatives from the community, the P.T.A., locally known civil rights leaders and black militants visit and keep close tabs on the school, looking for instances of incompetence, brutality, and breakdown in control. Teachers and administrators feel acutely the presence of the larger educational system and the restless and often angry community in their school. Rumors continually circulate as to the latest plans of Mrs. Jackson and Stratton.

Visited by journalists from local newspapers and representatives from TV, teachers then read about the innovative programs they are supposed to be initiating, the fine equipment in their new wing, and the exemplary relations amongst their integrated staff (Midway has nine black teachers). They observe their innovative lessons and their use of new equipment on the local TV news program. But they also read about the extensive sabotage and destruction of property that goes on in Midway and the low average reading scores that are published yearly in the newspapers. (Midway's children average two years behind the norm in reading scores and have the next to lowest reading average in the district.) When comparing notes with teachers from nearby schools at the local Jewish delicatessen, they are troubled by the poor reputation that Midway has in the district.

Midway's teachers are always rehashing school boycotts, wildcat strikes, incidents with black militants, flare-ups with the P.T.A., incidents of brutality with children, and teachers being attacked by children and parents—incidents that somehow never reached the press. Almost daily they read about and see televised accounts of conflicts between other ghetto schools and their communities similar to conflicts occurring in Midway School. They wonder when their school will become the focus of this crisis in ghetto education.

In 1954 the old Midway School was abandoned and the present building was occupied. For many years after that, Midway had a stable population of around 500 children—mostly Black—and 40 teachers. In recent years the school population grew to 800 and Midway became so overcrowded that the administration and the P.T.A. started lobbying for a new wing. Meanwhile, the school, which was almost entirely Black, began to absorb more and more Puerto Rican children. In the last few years the area north of the school has become almost entirely populated by Puerto Rican families so that the school serves as an informal boundary between the area of Randolph Park which is Black and Rogers Park which is Puerto Rican. At present Midway's population is about seventy-five per cent Black and twenty-five per cent Puerto Rican: in the lowest grades the ratio is fifty-fifty. It is thought that in a few years Midway will be a Puerto Rican school. In 1968 when the new wings were completed, the school population consisted of 1300 children and 70 teachers.

Midway's teachers are distinguished from each other primarily by the length of time they have taught. Their attitudes toward the school, toward new teachers, toward parents, toward children and toward themselves are shaped by the amount of teaching experience they've had at Midway School.

CHAPTER II

CHRONIC TEACHERS

ABOUT HALF of Midway's staff are chronic teachers. Having taught in the school from one to thirteen years, they have adopted a set of values and a style which enables them to operate with a minimum of personal discomfort. This relative ease is based, in part, on their ability to see their activity as consistent with their values. Chronic teachers accept the notion that control must precede education. But their acceptance of the necessity for control is intimately connected to the notion that they are "working *for* the children." Thus, a chronic teacher can hit a child and think it beneficial to the child. Recognizing no conflict between the administration's interest in "securing" the school and the interests of the children, he approaches his task with a minimum of self-consciousness.

This lack of self-consciousness is important in the chronic teacher's success with the children. The children are aware of his commitment. Whatever their opinions of his behavior, they respect his decisiveness and know that he will take any measure necessary to control them.

Legends of disciplinary virtuosity circulate throughout the teacher's world. One chronic teacher claimed that he never lost control of a class in ten years of teaching. When he lost control of a lunchroom one day, he almost quit. Another teacher has such a reputation for being "mean" that the children are too terrified to challenge his authority and he rarely has to apply the techniques for which he is so well known. A chronic teacher's image of his own competence is commensurate with his success in control.

Even among those disaffected teachers who theoretically reject the value of control, there is a practical interest in its mechanisms. Almost no one can feel above them. For regardless of a teacher's personal values, if he is unable to maintain control, he loses his self-esteem. The ability to control becomes a prerequisite for any sense of personal adequacy. Among male teachers it is a basic indicator of masculinity. Those chronic teachers who are virtuosos of control and tightness serve as models of adequacy to be emulated by other teachers.

Many male chronic teachers strut around the school with a military carriage and bearing. They dress impeccably and address their children in short staccato tones. They stand very straight in front of their classes, their eyes darting from side to side. When they enter a classroom, hallway, or lunchroom that is out of control, they act as if they had just entered a messy barracks. The more a male chronic teacher becomes known for his disciplinary competence, the more he exhibits the style of an army sergeant.

There are a few chronic teachers who can celebrate educational results. One teacher has frequent visits from former students, some of whom are in college. They remind him how much he taught them. But he is a rare exception. Most chronic teachers cannot afford to take educational results too seriously. If they should, they would have little basis for claiming personal success. So, they identify themselves with such terms as Professionalism, Experience, and Dedication which enable them to feel they are "teachers," and they involve themselves in administrative tasks and in the details of control. All of these involvements and identifications can be pursued apart from the issue of educational results.

The particular profile of chronic teachers' interests and (occupational) self-images does not protect them from the public definition that Midway is a "lousy" school. Neither success in control over students nor pride in one's own stalwart bearing insures self-satisfaction for the chronic teachers. In evaluating themselves by the "public" standard, they cannot separate the assessed quality of the school from their own assessed quality, and are thus in a defensive position in which their personal claims to competence are denied by the fact that the school is regarded as inferior.

The chronic teachers at Midway were trained and socialized during different periods in the recent history of the school. This history has spanned two administrations, each of which has left its own special stamp on those who had their formative experience in that period. These periods are known as the Kerner and Dobson Administrations. It is the quality of the chronic teacher that once he has become habituated to a style, he stays with this style irrespective of other changes in his immediate environment. Thus these chronic teachers resemble a kind of living archeology of the school's preceding administrations. It is of primary concern to us to see how these past generations of teachers mesh and clash with the present.

Kerner Generation Teachers

Those who have been teaching in Midway for five years or more are particularly distressed by the state of the school. They have seen Midway degenerate from "one of the best schools in the district" with "a strong principal" (Kerner) who "ran a tight school" to "one of the worst schools in the district." They sit in the teachers' lunchroom reminiscing about Kerner and certain classes they had during his administration.

It was a pleasure to teach these children. They were extremely cooperative and intelligent. They really wanted to learn. When I gave them an assignment they would act as if I were doing them a favor. They never caused me any trouble. They could even sense when I was not quite myself and would be especially considerate.

Every teacher from Kerner's administration had a class which represented the pinnacle of his career as a teacher.

They also tell of ideal relationships with the parents.

They took a positive interest in the school. Each year there was a science fair and a carnival which the parents helped us plan. Parents and children all came and we all had a wonderful time. And the parents supported the teachers. You didn't have to think it over every time you laid a hand on a child. It wasn't considered a racial thing if you hit a kid.

But of utmost importance is their image of Kerner.

All the teachers were on their toes always putting out their best because Kerner demanded it. When I first came to Midway I immediately realized that everybody was scared of Kerner. The teachers were just as scared of him as the children. And the children knew that the teachers were afraid of him so they knew that they had a reason to be. I was so scared of him that I didn't even sit at my desk for fear he would come popping in the door. I really put out for him and would do anything he would ask. Any teacher would, because they knew where their security in the school was coming from. You would send a kid to Kerner. He never caused you any trouble again. He was very strict but he was fair. If you were doing a job, he was appreciative and let you know it. But those teachers who weren't putting out, he rode them until they changed or left.

The spit and polish style of these Kerner generation teachers reflects their clinging to the historic past. The identification with the past enables them to uphold some sense of dignity in a situation where Midway School is decaying before their very eyes.

Kerner has departed, but his teachers still "put out" with the same intensity that they did for him. They are never late and rarely absent, using only about half of their allotted sick days. They volunteer for all sorts of crucial administrative tasks that are viewed by other teachers as "above and beyond the call of duty." One Kerner generation teacher supervises the lunchroom, the graduation exercises, and most of the assemblies. Another runs the school paper. Another sponsors the student council which elects school officers and organizes an annual talent show. They dominate the committees that plan and run the open houses, class teas, and other community events designed to bring about better relations with parents. Finally, they initiate and supervise the Open Horizon reading program, the after-school reading clinic, and other ameliorative programs. Kerner generation teachers perform a disproportionate amount of the work in Midway School.

In spite of their efforts to incorporate into Midway's program "the extra things that make a good school," the extracurricular activities "never quite come off the way they used to." The general deterioration of the school carries over to the special events. The children are not as well behaved, the parents are not as appreciative, and the other teachers are not as enthusiastic and willing to chip in as they were in the Kerner administration. Each event is followed by a *post mortem,* comparing the present to the Kerner administration. The more the Kerner generation teachers attempt to recapture the quality of the past, the greater their disappointment with the present.

Ultimately Kerner generation teachers come to despair for the state of the school and their positions in it. In spite of their personal careers which they view as successful and which parents and other teachers and administrators hold above reproach, they cannot enjoy the veneration. Some of them obtain transfers to other schools or become assistant principals or principals. Others get quasi-administrative or specialist jobs in the school such as librarian, remedial reading teacher, or lower-grade reading coordinator. One of these teachers would rather not come to school on days when many teachers are absent. She dreads being assigned to a regular class for the entire day. There are only five teachers from the Kerner administration left, and only one of them has a regular class.

Kerner generation teachers engage in desperate efforts to reinvoke the quality of Kerner's administration. Since there is no direct way to achieve this, they find alternate methods of adaptation. The taking of specialist jobs represents a form of orderly retreat from the classroom. Because they have seniority, they can at least be successful in preempting those positions that place the greatest possible distance between themselves and the children. They thus survive in the school even though they are living in the past.

Dobson Generation Teachers

Five years ago, about the time the population of the neighborhood began to increase sharply, Kerner was transferred to another district and after the short tenures of several intervening principals Dobson came in as the new principal. During the first two years of his administration, teachers could do what they pleased in their classes without fear that Dobson would pop into their classrooms, nor would he closely scrutinize lesson plans and other clerical work. "There was a relaxed atmosphere in the school. The teachers were left alone by administration and they did their job."

After two years of Dobson's administration and continued increases in the school population, two assistant principals, Ryley and Morton, were appointed. At this point the relationship of Dobson generation teachers to the administration abruptly changed. Morton became the supervisor for the upper-grade teachers and Ryley for the lower-grade teachers. They split up the other supervisory duties between them. What little previous contact Dobson had with his teachers greatly diminished. As he had not previously controlled his teachers, he did not attempt to control Ryley's and Morton's relationship with them. Adding this new administrative tier meant that the assistant principals defined relations between teachers and administrators.

Ryley and Morton demanded lesson plans regularly and promptly. They insisted that all other administrative tasks be completed in accordance with specified rules and timetables. While this posed no problem for Kerner generation teachers, Dobson generation teachers' inability or unwillingness to meet the deadlines were responded to by "nasty little notes" in the teachers' mail boxes and other varieties of reprimands.

The year after the assistant principals arrived, Mrs. Jackson was elected president of the P.T.A. She began a systematic harassment of teachers. Her small but lively clique would enter the school, "walk the halls," and check on the teachers to find out what was going on. Finding any infractions by teachers, Mrs. Jackson would "bring it up to Dobson" demanding that the teacher be "brought into line or fired." If she "did not get satisfaction" from Dobson she would "bring it up to Stratton." The teachers were terrified by Mrs. Jackson's harassment. They became extremely careful about what they said to other teachers and what they did in their classes. They were in continual fear for their jobs. Chronic teachers advised other teachers to "stay away from her" and "have nothing to do with her." As one teacher described Jackson, "She is anti-white, anti-Semitic, anti-everything."

The teachers' terror of Mrs. Jackson, however, is now mixed with a certain amount of fascination, for she is also a source of entertainment. Teachers urge each other to attend at least one P.T.A. meeting to "see the show." She is the constant object of jokes and humorous conversations. As they do with Stratton, Dobson, Ryley, and Morton, teachers imitate Mrs. Jackson's eccentricities and mannerisms. From the perspective of the teachers, Mrs. Jackson has the status of an administrator.

Mrs. Jackson's threatening policy recalls Kerner's tight supervision, but Dobson generation teachers lack a model to emulate or an experience to recapture. They prefer the calmness and tranquility of the early years of Dobson's administration. But unlike the Kerner generation teachers, they have no positive image of Midway School. They do not think of Midway as "their school."

Most of the thirty Dobson generation teachers have been assigned to Midway against their will, and because they hold regular teaching licenses have to remain in the school for at least five years. The goal of most of these teachers is to survive and "serve their time" until they can transfer out, hopefully to a white, middle-class school. They feel no loyalty to the school or its past. They have no psychological defenses to fall back upon that will enable them to feel any sense of pride in themselves as teachers at Midway. While they have learned the lessons of control, they feel angry about the demands of the administration (Ryley and Morton) and anxious about the incursions of the community (Mrs. Jackson) into their domains.

Chronic teachers have constructed their defenses from experiences they had during their formative periods. These defenses consist of withdrawal from the children, retreat into protected specialist jobs (for Kerner generation teachers), and in the case of the Dobson generation teachers, a hope for a better future in another school. Irrespective of the set of defenses selected, all allow that the chronic teacher must build a teaching style based on control. Once having mastered the technology of control the chronic teacher accepts control as the equivalent of teaching and absolves himself from any further self-conscious examination of his relationship to the children.

ABOUT HALF of Midway's staff are acute teachers, most of whom are products of an emergency summer program of college-level courses designed to alleviate the acute shortage of teachers in ghetto schools. Open to anyone with a college degree, the emergency program is paid for by the city and guarantees the untrained recruit a job in the fall. In exchange, the acute recruit has to sign a statement pledging to teach for a year.

The "open recruitment" of teachers attracts a mixed bag of applicants whose motives, interests, and ages are determined by a variety of factors not necessarily directly related to teaching.

Among the recruits who finally received positions at Midway, ten can be described as wishing to pursue a teaching career. Eight of them are women who have just graduated from college. Two are mothers in their forties whose children have grown up and who wish to begin or return to a teaching career. Some of these more career-minded teachers actually want to teach in a ghetto school.

The rest of the acute teachers are primarily motivated by their desire not to be drafted. They enrolled in the emergency summer program because it offered them the opportunity to avoid the war in Vietnam. Several afternoon sessions of the training program were devoted entirely to convincing the 1000 or more draft-age men that their draft deferments would be forthcoming upon completion of their training and assignment to a school.

The vast majority of acute teachers are just out of college, graduate schools, and previous jobs which did not offer them protection from the war. Thus, young aspiring lawyers, accountants, businessmen, and graduate students in psychology, sociology, political science, and history comprise a major block of teachers at Midway. After being in the school for a short time, these teachers come to feel that they are doing a form of alternate service not too different from their fantasies about Vietnam. They often joke about the advantages and disadvantages of the two alternatives. In view of their experience with the children, the war imagery can take on a reality which an outsider could not imagine to be appropriate to a school. After particularly bad days in the classroom, these acute teachers congregate and compare their difficulties with the children. The teacher having the most difficulty with his class is soothed with the comment, "At least it's not as bad as Vietnam."

In spite of their questionable motives for coming to Midway and the forced or tentative nature of their commitment, many acute teachers would like to do a good job. In their own and others' eyes, they would like to be successful. Many want good references for future jobs. Almost all would like to feel that they were earning their pay.

The Ameliorative Impulse

Acute teachers initially express no public disdain for Black or Puerto Rican children. Indeed, many acute teachers pride themselves on their liberal and progressive politics, their opposition to the war in Vietnam, and their support of the War on Poverty and other ameliorative programs. Some of the graduate students see themselves as budding college professors, intellectuals, and social critics. A few have read Paul Goodman and would like to change the school system. Several have been active in the civil rights movement and would like to continue their civil rights activities as teachers. A few have had jobs in welfare, social work, and poverty programs. These latter are less optimistic about achieving their political goals in the school.

When the acute teachers arrive at Midway, their basic sympathies are with the children and the parents. They would like to "reach out to" or "make it" with the children whom they view as "disadvantaged" individuals to be "helped" through "sensitive and creative teaching." But these humanistic intentions and sympathies are not, in most instances, based on personal experience with ghetto inhabitants. Acute teachers have learned about the ghetto from newspapers, magazines, TV, movies, and books. Their sympathies have been cultivated in suburbs and universities which are totally divorced from the objects of the sympathy. They assume they can successfully apply their suburban and academic morality to Midway School.

The Rhetoric of Orientation

Before being assigned to a school, these good-intentioned acute teachers are given a brief orientation in the district office by the district superintendent:

We have called this meeting to accomplish three goals. We would like to tell you what our district is like. We would like to assign you to a school which is closest to your home. And we want to personally welcome you to the district. District 7 has eighteen elementary schools, four junior high schools and two high schools. It encompasses the Rogers Park and Randolph Park areas. In this district we have a very active community and school board which is interested in only one thing—good schools and good teachers. We have in District 7 the support of the community. Now the principals in District 7 do not think that they are God's answer to education. They are down to earth, accessible, and want to do everything in their power to help you new teachers to have a satisfying and successful experience.

Now we do have problems in our schools. However you will be happy to teach in this district. You will not be afraid to come to any school in this district. There has not been any picketing. We are happy that the community is behind us. So now that we have cleared up any misconceptions you might have about the district, we can turn to more technical matters.

First of all, I have to tell you something that may disturb many of you. Those of you who are from the high school part of the emergency summer training program, I have to tell you that you will be teaching elementary school. There are just no vacancies in the secondary schools and we only have vacancies in the elementary schools. Now if you can get some secondary school outside the district to request you I will release you. But if for any other reason you wish to change to another district I will not release you. Now I know that many of our high school people who are young men will take the assignment because of the draft. I will not go further into this.

The superintendent conveys to the acute teachers that problems which occur in the district are not occurring, and reminds them of the consequences of refusing the assignment.

Upon being assigned to Midway, acute teachers are informed by chronic teachers that almost everything they were told by Superintendent Stratton and his assistant Golden is the opposite of what actually exists in the school. Chronic teachers say that "the school is in a state of complete chaos," that "Dobson doesn't do anything but sit in his office," that "all Morton and Ryley do is tell the teachers to meet deadlines and send them notes when they don't," and that "Mrs. Jackson wants to fire all of the white Jewish teachers" and "take over the school":

> The administration will attempt to hide and gloss over a lot of problems in the school, but you will find out soon enough how difficult the children will be and what you will have to do to survive.

Interspersed between these conversations with chronic teachers are formal orientation conferences with the administration:

> Morton: Now I'm just going to say a few important things until the principal comes in. School will be on three different sessions because the new wing is not completed. Now one of the most important things in getting started is the establishment of routines for the children and for yourself. Now you're going to have problem children—children who will give you trouble. The minute you have a problem you can't expect us to immediately do something about it. But you can keep a file on him, an anecdotal record, and if patterns emerge, we'll eventually take care of it. Now of course the instructors in the universities say "be creative with the children," "work with them," "love them." But this cannot be accomplished without routines and we expect you to concentrate on this aspect.

(Dobson is introduced)

> Dobson: You constitute almost half of our present staff and we have the job of making you into teachers. It takes anywhere from three to five years to become a teacher. Some make it in less. Your first year of teaching will be the most difficult job you will have in your life. Plan books are to be submitted every two weeks. Sometimes they will have comments on them. Sometimes they will have few or none. We will read them carefully or casually, depending on the individual involved or the situation. The purpose of the plan book is to see that you have a plan and

cover the curriculum so that you know what you are doing. The children will do everything in their power to confuse you, take advantage of you, obstruct your teaching until you are firm with them—until you let them know that you know what you are doing. We have one guidance counselor and referral is made to her through the supervisors. But remember you are responsible for classroom discipline. The more you have to call a supervisor for help, the less efficient you are in classroom control. You are to use anything and everything to maintain classroom control except physical violence. First of all, it's against the law. Also, parents are sensitive to any physical violence and children will sometimes tell their parents. No matter what a parent tells you, even if she says, "Give him a good beating," never lay a hand on a child in anger because there can be repercussions. It's all right to put your arm around a child if you have established rapport with him or if it is an appropriate situation for touching him—putting your arm around him in a friendly way.

Even stronger is the chronic teacher's stress on the overriding necessity for control.

A lot of new teachers, well, they want to be very idealistic— want to be a buddy to the kids—have a nice relaxed atmosphere in the classroom. Well, if you do that the kids will destroy you. You've got to be firm at the beginning, keep them busy, organize the routines. Don't take any nonsense. Then, after a while you can accomplish something and let up later. But if you start off on the wrong track, it will take you maybe a whole year to control the class. The first few weeks, if you accomplish nothing but control, you are doing a job.

Thus, the acute teacher is advised that his inability to control the children will be taken as evidence of his inadequacy as a teacher. The teacher who loses control becomes dependent on other teachers and administrators to regain it. But other teachers resent having to "stop whatever they are doing" to help a teacher "break up a fight," "remove a child from a classroom," "take a disruptive child to the office," or "quiet down a class." The teacher who relies heavily on other teachers and administrators for the solution of his problems with children gets a reputation for incompetence. He is thought to be "not doing a job." All his humanitarian dreams, liberal ideas, and sympathetic inclinations are redefined as the basis of failure. His commitment to becoming competent, to being self-sufficient in his work, to working for his pay, and to his self-image as a white-collar professional is threatened by the prospect that those teaching methods demanded of him will be inconsistent with his personal morality.

The practical education of the acute teacher begins when he observes at first hand how children are treated at Midway. He sees them being marched around the hallways. In a *controlled* classroom, they sit in their seats with their hands folded, go to the blackboard, clean up the floor, get their coats, put them away, clean the erasers, sharpen pencils, line up straight, two by two. The typical teacher gives commands in a stentorian voice. Often he shouts them. The volume of the commands increases in relation to the degree that they are not being followed. When commands and shouts do not work, he uses the hand or the stick. He "knocks heads." To the acute teacher it looks like what he had imagined boot camp might be like.

The military techniques and the methods of violence that he observes conflict with the moral codes of his own academic and suburban past. He views them as ethically and aesthetically repugnant. The acute teacher finds himself in the position of being expected to participate in activities for which he would immediately condemn himself as well as others. Nevertheless he must face the practical problem of teaching the children. The children severely test his ability to hold to his previous values.

The Effort to Bargain with the Children

In spite of the warning and example of administrators and

chronic teachers, an acute teacher is likely to attempt a soft line with the children. He may greet his class informally, not demand that they keep a perfectly straight line to the classroom, and not try immediately to establish rigid routines. He allows the children drinks of water and trips to the bathroom. He does not immediately clamp down when the children attempt to talk to each other, leave their seats, or leave the classroom. He may even look the other way when he observes children eating in class. He initiates a policy in keeping with his liberal ideology that enables him to sustain his feelings of moral superiority over the chronic teachers.

He may assume that if given a certain amount of leeway, the children will recognize his partiality toward them. He hopes that the children will reciprocate by appreciating his humanitarian efforts. The teacher's easy-going approach is an indirect plea to the children for exemption from the battle over control.

The Acute Teacher is Destroyed

The children do not take up the bargain on his terms. Seeing that the teacher is not concerned with a straight line, the children dispense with the line. If he fails to clamp down on talking, eating, and moving around, the children talk, eat, move, and leave the classroom as much as possible. Children see the liberal policy not as an invitation to participate in a well-mannered civilized classroom, but as an opportunity to realize objectives of their own. The acute teacher is at first not aware that the children may have their own objectives.

Still the acute teacher's liberalism is conditional on the children's empathy toward his problem. He expects the children to be as sensitive to his problem as he feels he is to their problem. He reacts angrily to their lack of appreciation and unwillingness to uphold their end of the bargain. He feels personally betrayed and begins to shout at the children, demanding that they keep quiet, stay in their seats, and stop eating. The demands are ineffective, for he had granted these freedoms previously. So the teacher must begin to threaten. He threatens to send a child to the principal's office, write a letter home to his mother, or have him suspended. He may chase a child around the room, pound his fist on the table or threaten to hit him. With each betrayal of the teacher's sense of decency and fairness, he depends more and more on the very "indecent" techniques he previously condemned.

But the shouting and threatening fail to pacify the children. For they are cognizant of the teacher's inexperience. They are furthermore aware that his permissive policy has been an experiment. The children distinguish between acute and chronic teachers' use of techniques. The shouts and threats are not part of a disciplinary plan but merely an emotional response to the situation. Thus, the children regard attempts at control as a loss of control. They experience the loss of control as a higher form of victory than the freedom to eat, talk, or move around. The more the teacher screams at the children, pounds his fist on the table, and chases them around the room, the greater their delight in the victory.

The children are delighted because they are invulnerable. The teacher is making all sorts of threats he has no intention of carrying out. They are extremely sensitive to the discrepancy between threats and action. The discrepancy is established by calling a series of bluffs. The rebel leader tests the teacher to see how far he can go without being punished. If the teacher backs down the rebel leader ups the ante. The called bluff and the upped ante define for the less courageous children the level on which they can safely pursue their disobedience. If the rebel leader screams at the teacher and gets away with it, the other children feel they can talk to each other without consequence. If he runs around the room, they get out of their seats and walk around. If he starts a fight, they run around the room. Soon all the children, even those who are usually obedient, start leaving their seats, getting drinks, talking, screaming, fighting, eating—anything that is at least one degree less extreme than the rebel leader's activity.

Finally, all commands are useless. The teacher gives orders knowing they are not going to be obeyed. The children know that he acknowledges his impotence. Each escalation in shouting, stamping, and pounding is seen by the children as a further admission of impotence. It takes ever more extreme measures to get a response from them because they immediately become accustomed to the current level of escalation as the norm. The more the teacher escalates, the more he establishes his impotence.

The teacher's awareness of his impotence finally precipitates a desperate act. After shouting at the children with no apparent results or just staring at them for a few minutes, he suddenly grabs a child and makes an example of him in front of the class by dragging him across the room, twisting his arm, grabbing him on the back of the neck, or hitting him on the shoulder or face. He may even drag him out of the room to an administrator's office and deposit him there.

Control in the classrooms of some acute teachers breaks down to the point where the teacher feels like a cop in a ghetto riot. Fights break out. Books, spitballs, thumbtacks, paper airplanes, paper clips, food, and chairs fly across the room. Occasionally, children consciously caricature a riot. They stage elaborate fights, organize group chanting, and sing dirty songs for the teachers' benefit. Regardless of the intensity of the disruption, the children never lose sight of the teacher's response. Their delight in their activity is directly proportional to his desperation.

In the process of losing control, frenzied teachers lose all perspective. Their faces get red and puffed. Their clothing is rumpled and covered with chalk dust. At times, classes and teachers become completely hysterical. In the midst of the hysteria, a teacher may beg the children for a few minutes of peace. Another may try a number of things in rapid succession, hoping that one of them will work. First he screams at the children. Then he makes a joke. Then he appeals to their guilt. Then he begs again. Some are driven to tears. Finally he makes an example of someone. The more hysterical the teacher becomes the more desperately random his behavior.

The children's energy and staying power is limitless. With each hysterical outburst the children appear more confident in their disobedience and intent on their rebellion. Very rapidly the acute teacher is physically and emotionally exhausted.

The acute teacher responds to his loss of control with feelings of personal inadequacy and unworthiness. Among men, these feelings border on anxiety about their masculinity. They begin to compare themselves unfavorably to the chronic male teachers who strut around the school. Among certain teachers the initial experience with the children is destructive to the point where previous successes, financial, academic, occupational, and erotic, temporarily lose their salience. They talk about their inability to sleep nights worrying about what the children are going to do to them the following day. Their experience in Midway School causes deep personal fear, even terror.

The sense of being destroyed is accompanied by an awareness that they are reneging on their intentions to be human with the children and their desire to be a respectable professional. The anger felt toward the children for not allowing them to live out their liberal ideas and be a good teacher is complicated by an awareness of using "chronic techniques." At different points for different teachers a sharp battle line is eventually drawn between themselves and the children.

For the teacher, the crucial issue is then defined as who is going to be destroyed. One put it tightly, "It's them or us." Reluctantly, the teacher then must admit that he is beginning to brutalize the children. If brutalization of the children (and himself) is seen as the only basis for survival and guilt is the only possible response to his brutalizing, the acute teacher is destroyed.

In actual fact twenty-one of the thirty-five acute teachers were "destroyed." In educational circles outside of Midway School the term "being destroyed" is defined as "failure" because the teacher becomes "personally involved" and is unable to control his class. The phrase "being destroyed" conforms to usage at Midway School where everyone knows personally many examples of teachers who were driven to the verge of madness before they began to give up the teaching methods which they hoped would be consistent with their ethical and moral standards. Under ordinary circumstances some of these teachers would have quit their jobs and left Midway. But as devastating as their experience is, Midway as a way of life is thought to be a better alternative than Vietnam. They wish to avoid Vietnam for the same ideological reasons that they hope to avoid the methods of the chronic teachers. Thus when their own teaching methods don't work, and they feel destroyed, the acute teachers react as if they had been sent to Vietnam and look for any means to survive.

Closing Ranks with the Chronic Teachers

Previous to their initial encounter with the children, chronic teachers were objects of moral indignation for acute teachers. Initial observations of chronic teachers at work confirmed their preconceptions about the quality of teachers in ghetto schools. But now, contact with the children has made it difficult for acute teachers to sustain an unambivalently critical attitude toward those teachers whose advice and warnings about their relationships to the children have turned out to be so accurate.

Teachers who, a few days earlier, criticized and condemned the "immoral" activity of the chronic teachers, actively seek their advice. Desperate acute teachers buttonhole well-known chronic teachers in the teachers' lunchroom, the halls, and the general office, to seek information as to how they can gain control and prevent their own destruction. Chronic teachers are generous and explicit with their advice. They view the interest in their techniques as a further indication of their competence, and a vindication of their position toward the children.

Acute teachers seek the ear of other acute teachers who they hope will not moralize about their behavior with the children. To his relief the acute teacher discovers that many others are having similar problems. Whenever the opportunity arises, acute teachers congregate in the lunchroom, the office, the halls, and outside their classrooms to relieve each other of their burdens.

The mutual confessions often become contests. The object is to determine who is having the greatest difficulty with the children. Teachers claim that they have been more totally destroyed and have taken more drastic counter-measures than any other teacher. Through competitive confessions the acute teachers exempt each other from any moral accountability for their actions with the children. Add to this the advice-seeking from chronic teachers, and the acute teacher has taken the first hesitant steps toward a redefinition of his *modus operandi* in the school.

Once the acute teacher realizes the impracticality and self-destructive effects of his ethical standards, the emphasis of his activity rapidly shifts from attempting to maintain the standards to developing a method by which he can survive. Only when experience forces the acute teacher to loosen the moral inhibitions of his past can he hope to attain the "experience" necessary to becoming a "competent" teacher. Having learned that control is synonymous with education and now being willing to try anything to establish control, he has adopted the very moral psychology he would have needed to survive in Vietnam.

CHAPTER IV

THE ANATOMY OF CONTROL

UPON FIRST ARRIVING at Midway, acute teachers are overwhelmed with the rhetoric of control. All the orientation conferences with administrators and bull-sessions with chronic teachers stress the overriding priority of classroom discipline and order in the halls. The central theme of these orientation conferences is that if a teacher is "firm" and "knows what he is doing" control will take care of itself. Even in the bull-sessions with chronic teachers there is much talk about the consequences of losing control but not much said about the specific techniques for its maintenance. Listening to Dobson and Morton describe the process of achieving control in terms of "thorough planning," "interesting lessons," "being consistent," "establishing rapport," "taking anecdotal records," and "being professional," the acute teacher is somewhat mystified and unsure of what is expected of him.

However, after being in Midway for only a short time and observing how chronic teachers and administrators treat the children, the acute teacher realizes that most of the effective methods for control are publicly defined as immoral if not illegal and thus cannot be discussed at Midway's staff meetings. Likewise, chronic teachers are at first hesitant to discuss their methods with those new recruits who, in their idealistic statements about how they plan to treat the children, imply a criticism of chronic methods and appear to take a morally superior attitude toward chronic teachers. Thus the acute teacher's initial self-righteousness and the "illegal" and "immoral" nature of those activities he is self-righteous about prevent him from learning the real strategies of control.

When describing to colleagues their proven skills and any combination of useful disciplinary options, teachers refer to these skills and options as "the system." Teachers refer to using these options directly with children as "playing the system." In effect, establishing control means "playing the system."

Once the acute teacher realizes that he cannot survive in Midway unless he controls his class and that survival is preferred to moral purity, he suppresses his moral scruples and begins to play the system. Through the experience of being destroyed, the absorption of advice from chronic teachers, the sharing of experience with other acute teachers, and trial and error, most acute teachers acquire those skills necessary to intermittently maintain a minimal degree of control. While it is possible that few if any teachers are aware of or utilize all the possibilities and dimensions of "the system," it is our concern here to describe the entire system that Midway's teachers play.

"Not Taking It Personally"

Confronted with the children's irreverence and disobedience the acute teacher responds with anger and deep feelings of personal inadequacy and unworthiness. He takes it personally. In not being able to fulfill his image of an educator and becoming instead an object of ridicule and a source of entertainment for the children, he experiences his humiliation directly and intimately. In the act of failing he reacts as if the failure were happening *to* him.

Previous to and during this period of destruction, the acute teacher is warned by chronic teachers and administrators that when he "takes it personally," "gets involved," and allows the children to "get to him," the children will intensify the very behavior that got him "involved" in the first place. The experienced advisors add that when children exploit a teacher's "weak spot," the exploitation is not directed against him as a person but only as a teacher. Since the teacher is only a symbol anyway, and since personal responses to the children make teaching unbearable, the teacher is encouraged not to respond as a person. Midway encourages the acute recruit to show as little emotion as possible, detach himself from his own destruction and act as if it were not happening to him. This is what Midway's teachers mean by "not taking it personally."

Eventually, acute teachers realize the impracticality of their emotional responses. They learn to ignore all attempts of children to elicit a personal response. Children are often disappointed when viewing a teacher who is in the process of becoming impersonal. When all efforts at eliciting the rants and raves fail, they may beg the teacher to "get mad." By disengaging himself and hence becoming able to respond to the children's baiting in bland and unrewarding ways, the teacher sours the children's sense of victory. Once having achieved this coolness under fire, the acute teacher can begin to choose appropriate responses and apply them more effectively. Self-control and impersonality are necessary prerequisites for establishing control.

"Setting up Routines"

The object of routines is to fill time safely. The more the enterprising teacher can involve his children in routines, the less likely they are to threaten his control. For the nature of the routines themselves prevents all sorts of activity that might otherwise take place.

In many classes the typical day is filled up with a succession of marches to the classrooms, hanging-up of coats, pledges to the flag, watering of plants, checking of homework, handing out paper, collecting papers, trips to the bathroom, getting drinks of water. The succession of activities is governed by rules which specify when and how they are to be done. The detailed specifications of what *can* be done have the effect of defining what *cannot* be done.

Many chronic teachers become involved in the aesthetics of their routines. One teacher disliked her children coming straight forward from their seats to her desk. She claimed it blocked her vision and upset her concentration. She now has her children walk to the back of the room, around all the desks, and approach her desk from the side. Another teacher spends much of her time perfecting already established routines. Her children are controlled enough not to get out of their seats or talk without permission. So now, her major concern is *how* they sit (straight back), stand in line (at attention), and pledge to the flag (right hand over the *heart*, not the belly). She maintains that her class "almost runs by itself."

By refining routines and thus "tightening up" their classes, teachers protect themselves from the loss of control, present themselves as experienced professionals, and establish their superiority over other teachers.

Economy of Force

The effective use of routines presumes the teacher has the power to enforce them. When children challenge the teacher's power, it is crucial that they be defeated. So, on the first day of school a teacher picks out the potential rebel leader, and, at the first sign of disobedience, makes an example of him. He grabs the disobedient child and threatens to beat him up if he doesn't stop what he is doing. In many instances he smacks the child in front of the class. If the leader is decisively defeated, other children are less likely to rebel.

Many teachers are proud of the technique of example-making. They say that they are using minimum force to establish control. They stress the importance of establishing "who's boss" on the first day. "A little muscle" guarantees that they "won't have to be knocking heads all year." They compare themselves favorably with those teachers who "start off wrong" and end up "hitting the children ten times as much as I do." Many conclude that by defeating the children early and decisively they are actually doing them a favor.

One teacher can hit a child so rapidly on the back of the head or ear that the act is barely observable. He can teach a lesson in front of the class, swiftly walk to the back of the room, and hit the child without breaking the rhythm of the lesson. Other teachers discuss with each other the finer points of striking children by using pressure points and the ways of causing a child considerable pain without appearing to do so. Like those who stress routines, there are teachers who make an aesthetic of force.

The more a teacher convinces himself that skillful violence brings control, the less inhibited he becomes in its use. The opportunity for the prolonged use of force usually occurs when the initial battle is not as decisive as hoped. It often drags on for weeks. The teachers, having used their ultimate weapons, find that they must use it repeatedly to maintain control. Some teachers come to expect a prolonged engagement in which they must be prepared to administer a continuous barrage of "slaps on the face," "pinches on the neck," "whacks on the behind," and "knocked heads." Some teachers claim they will hit a child in the beginning "even if he looks like he is about to do something wrong." Even teachers who expect an extended battle with the children justify violence by pointing to its long-term results. As one teacher concluded, "They finally learned that I meant business."

Force is so crucial to Midway's stability and its staff's security that many teachers become fixated on the technologies of violence and literally prevent chaos in the classroom by the effective use of terror.

Buck-passing and Delegating Authority

If a teacher is unable to maintain control through routines backed up by violence, he has other options open to him. He can request the aid of an administrator or another teacher. For example, an acute teacher was having a particularly difficult time with a class. He called for Mr. Morton. When Morton arrived the children were screaming, running around the room, and throwing school supplies at each other.

> Morton: Okay, everyone quiet and in their seats. I want to see everyone sitting and folding their hands. Now Mr. Miller has told me that he is very disappointed in the class this afternoon. He said that he was very happy about the morning class, but you have been very bad. Now you have one hour left in the day, and you can get a commendation if you are very good the rest of the day. Who would like a commendation to your regular teacher? (All of the children raise their hands.) Well, then I want you to remain like this for the rest of the day.

For the remaining hour Mr. Miller, with minimum success, copied Morton's approach, reminding the children all the while that they might get a special commendation.

The teacher can also send disobedient children into the halls, to the class of another teacher, or to the office of an administrator. Expelled children roam the halls, bang on classroom doors, invade other classrooms, and harass the infuriated teacher. One teacher sent twelve of his children to twelve different classes every day. Eventually the other teachers realized what he was doing and refused to take any of his children. Any significant degree of buck-passing rapidly earns a teacher a reputation for not doing his job. An overreliance on administrators and colleagues in maintaining discipline destroys for the teacher the possibility of establishing his own authority on his own terms. It also leads to resentment by other teachers and failure in the classroom.

Many teachers write letters to the parents of "disruptive children." An acute teacher quickly discovers that if he writes a letter home, the child is usually docile the following day. The child usually gets a beating from his parents. Certain teachers refuse to hit the children. They are sensitive about using corporal punishment. Yet many of them are in control of their classes. On a given day they send from one to ten letters home to parents. When asked to defend their activity in the face of their belief that teachers should not hit children, they often reply that it is the duty of the teacher to inform the parent when the child is bad, and they have no control over the parents. The teacher can take credit for the control without assuming responsibility for the means by which it is achieved. This is perhaps the only variety of successful buck-passing available to the teacher.

Children are also used as an instrument of control. Each class has a child who is bigger and stronger than the rest. Some teachers appoint the strongest child "class president," and make him responsible for control. In a few classes the teacher can be seen sitting relaxed at his desk while the class president and his assistants, called "monitors," walk around the room with rulers threatening and smacking the children when they get out of line. To avoid hitting the children themselves or for efficiency's sake, the teacher delegates the dirty work. Instead of buck-passing, this teacher becomes a high and distant arbiter who occupies the throne.

Occasionally class presidents become so imbued with their own sense of power that they continue to discipline the children after the teacher has told them to stop. One teacher found that her class president was abusing his authority so much that she had to depose him, or the authority of the throne itself would have been at stake. The embittered child then used his skills to stir up the other children against her. The use of the child disciplinarians is ultimately ineffective unless the teacher is willing to discipline the child disciplinarian.

Bribery, Praise, and the Use of Curriculum

Children are tempted with parties, snacks, trips to the toilet, trips away from school, and extra art and music periods if they are good. Or, if they are bad, scheduled gym and library periods, planned parties and trips are cancelled.

Often the bribery becomes abstract and takes the form of praise which, while lacking any tangible material benefit, is highly valued by the children. Children are reminded by substitute teachers that a "good report" or a "special commendation" will be given to their regular teacher if they behave. In some classes the teachers have a star and zero system. The children are rewarded and punished solely on that basis. One teacher, after going through a prolonged process of destruction, adopted a point system. The children are rewarded points for doing assigned work and keeping quiet. At the end of the week he announces to a hushed class the total number of points that each child has earned. Another teacher stands in front of his class and puts down a mark on the blackboard for each minute that the class is disruptive. For each disruptive minute, the class has to stay a minute after school. When the children have built up a back-log of minutes, he tells them that for each minute of quiet, he will take a minute off the after-school penalty. The more involved the children become in contests over stars, points, and minutes, the less they contest being controlled.

Many teachers do little in their classes but run the children through a series of bribes. The use of bribes is viewed by these teachers as less morally objectionable and less physically and emotionally taxing than screaming, sending letters home, or hitting. At the same time the teacher is aware that he is putting something over on the children. Of course none of the points, stars, good reports, or special commendations have any material effect on a child's future. They are never recorded in the permanent record book along with the objective reading and math scores which follow him throughout his educational career. Yet "star" and "point" systems work better than promises of trips, parties, and cookies. Teachers are often amazed at how seriously children will work for token praise.

Another instrument of control is the educational curriculum. The teacher finds a simple task, such as copying words or sentences off the blackboard or looking up words in the dictionary. Such tasks, which involve no teaching and often allow the teacher to sit at his desk, may involve the children for as long as two hours. A teacher who uses a technique like this is aware that such tasks have no educational value, but they do control without brutalizing. A few teachers put their work on the board in cycles. When they finish one cycle a month long (sometimes only a week long), they start over. They claim that the children do not remember what was previously on the board and are surprised that children will involve themselves in tasks they view as meaningless.

Regardless of the historical period in which they are trained and the political values and moral scruples they bring to the school, control eventually becomes the major task of Midway's teachers. At different points after varying degrees of resistance, Midway's teachers approach their task with a determination and attention to detail which suggests the quality of a foot soldier, his rifle, and his terrain. While some teachers justify their military preparedness with the notion that control is a prerequisite for education, and that the enemy will be made free through combat, others merely express their concern with survival and leave the question of military purpose to the generals and the politicians. A few teachers maintain that their survival does not depend on educating the children but on "containing them." No matter what educational views they hold, Midway's teachers know that their general well-being, sense of personal adequacy, and self-worth, confidence of masculinity, and knowledge of professional competence rapidly decline when they lose control. The personal anxieties aroused in a teacher by the prospect of loss of control is a much more salient source of motivation than is the realization that the children's education may be inadequate.

Midway provides its teachers with a system of disciplinary techniques and administrative options for survival on the job. While most of these techniques are publicly immoral and formally illegal, teachers justify their use by declaring that "it's part of the job." When they say this, they mean that regardless of the public definition of their activity and their personal views toward what they do, anyone who calls himself a teacher engages in these activities if he expects to remain in the school. Teachers further admonish parents and administrators for their hypocrisy in demanding law and order in the school and then looking askance at the means by which it is achieved.

At any one time, few if any teachers are aware of the total logic of "the system" or the complete range of opportunities available to them. They are aware only of particular aspects of the system that seem to work. Usually acute teachers do not let other teachers know that they are aware of a system until they start playing it. As one enthusiastic convert remarked:

> I must have been crazy to take all that shit. No more! I sent twenty letters home last week. Morton took Robert out of my class. Yesterday I kept them after school for an hour. It's the system. There is no other way. You've got to play the system.

Only after the acute teacher has been destroyed many times,

has experimented with various techniques, and has observed other teachers using routines, violence, children, parents, administrators, bribes, and curriculum with varying degrees of success and failure does he discover the system's rationality. He now sees the possibility of calculating responses to hypothetical situations that he knows he must face. He is now motivated to learn fully the anatomy of control and dedicates himself to this new learning experience in ways that would validate any on-the-job training program. He finds what works and learns by doing. Each day this experimenting teacher discovers a new dimension to the system and a new extension of its rationality. At this point some acute teachers discuss the possibilities of playing the system as an exercise in philosophical discourse.

A chronic teacher eventually focuses on a repertoire of techniques which provide him with a degree of efficiency so that experimentation is no longer necessary. At this point he uses his options and responds to situations almost automatically. His techniques for maintaining control have become so refined that he becomes a technician pure and simple and loses contact with those aspects of the system which he himself does not use. Thus he may be less aware of its total breadth than the acute teacher who constantly innovates in his search for a method of control.

Midway's teachers act individually with the intention of preventing their own destruction and not of maintaining general control. But in taking those measures which make their life bearable in Midway, they also do a job for the school. As each teacher evolves those tactics that allow him to survive, he unwittingly contributes to the unavoidable process of general control.

CHAPTER V

THE STRAIN
TOWARD CHRONICITY

FAMILIARITY with a system of control and practical experience in its use doesn't necessarily solve the acute teacher's problem. For the very qualities of flexibility and self-consciousness which allow him to rapidly acquaint himself with the mechanisms of control prevent him from immediately casting off the moral systems of his suburban and academic past. Every time the acute teacher ruminates on methods he has applied in the classroom or intends to apply (which such a short time before he viewed as morally inapplicable), even as he enjoys the aesthetic qualities of his new-found system and marvels at its practical results, he cannot help but apply his previous ethical system to the present one. So that harsh judgments on his activity enter his consciousness every time he reflects on the system he is currently learning to play. For the acute teacher who takes his past seriously, there is no easy solution. In actuality, knowledge of Midway's system exacerbates his moral problem.

Drawing the Line

Thus, even after the initial period of destruction and learning the system, some acute teachers are unable to play the system in a consistent and rational way. When they are being destroyed, they resort to traditional control tactics on an *ad hoc* basis. They shout, threaten, bribe, and hit; anything to get themselves through a desperate situation. But tough tactics do not become morally acceptable through use. Even after being repeatedly destroyed by the children and giving in to tactics they feel to be immoral, these teachers adhere to the belief that the children "should not be brutalized."

Each teacher has a line beyond which he will not go. A few refuse to touch a child, no matter what. Others may grab a child and hold him or even twist his arm or pinch his neck, but they refuse to actually hit him. Others refuse to send letters home because they feel that it would be the same as hitting the children. Finally, some fail to report children's infractions to the administrators because they fear that the child might be suspended. By refusing to participate in activities that are particularly odious, the less odious acts become acceptable and the teacher salvages some sense of self-justification.

All teachers at Midway have a calculus by which they justify themselves in situations where they are aware of their moral vulnerability. Chronic teachers dwell on their success at control to counteract the feeling that they are not teaching the children anything. Teachers who feel that they actually teach the children something focus on this to counteract the feeling that they are not getting results on objective tests. But for acute teachers who have difficulty in controlling their classes, "teaching the children something" is not an issue. They try to justify their existence in the school by claiming that they (unlike other teachers) do not brutalize the children.

Acute teachers' efforts at avoiding being destroyed continually interfere with their efforts at avoiding brutalization. Many discover that in order to survive they have to redraw the line several times each day. A teacher makes a pact with himself that he is not going to shout at the children. But he immediately dispenses with this because talking softly doesn't work.

Then shouting at the children is viewed as a lesser evil than grabbing at them. So, to avoid grabbing the children the teacher screams his lungs out. But soon, shouting no longer works. He begins grabbing the children. Grabbing also has a limited effectiveness. So the teacher ends up hitting. Every time he uses a technique that he would have been ashamed of using the day before, he becomes aware that he is violating standards that only yesterday were inviolable. Because he has "moral standards," each new escalation in his brutalization of the children is accompanied by increased self-repugnance.

Since he resents being made to feel guilty, the harassed teacher often ends up using abhorrent control tactics in an extreme way. He yells louder, grabs and hits the children more often, and harder than do the chronic teachers who have learned the economics of force.

In some cases where the ethical tenets of the teacher's past were not taken so seriously, the restraints of liberal morality are completely abandoned. When this happens, the brutalizing suggests the rhythm of a military prison. And the teacher begins to justify his brutalization on the grounds that the children are "inferior," "stupid," "like animals," and hence either deserve to be brutalized or do not mind it.

Once he takes this decisive step in his consciousness, he uses parents, administrators, other teachers, children, threats, praise, bribes, and violence in all their variety and in any combination in a crash program to control the children. Having opted for a new ideology he can now play the system with a vengeance.

These teachers now begin to take a certain pride in their disciplinary ability. The pride and sense of power is accompanied by a feeling of relaxation and sense of security. They begin to feel that they might be able to last out the year after all and perhaps make it until they are twenty-six. They have become the drill sergeants they were so anxious to avoid in the army.

The Awareness of Betrayal

However, because liberal ideology is not that easy to cast off, most acute teachers are unable to rid themselves entirely of discomforting moral reflection. Relieved to get out of the classroom and into the teachers' lunchroom, the teacher compares his experience with his fellow teachers and takes some comfort that he is not alone in his collusion against the children. But when he leaves the school, his moral values become more pronounced. The farther he gets from the experience, the more he judges himself in moral terms. He feels guilty and vows to change. But when he returns to the school, the need to survive takes precedence again. He is conscious of betraying the children only when he is in no position to betray them.

Other teachers, however, are not able to compartmentalize their morality. One teacher, ineffective in control, depends on bribery as a means of survival. He gives the children cookies and then asks them to be good, lets them go home early if they behave, and is extremely generous with special commendations, good reports, stars, and Mickey Mouse points. But he describes to other teachers his disgust at being so manipulative. At the same time he views what he is doing as absurd. His sharply worded commands are always accompanied by a barely visible smile in the corner of his mouth. Teachers like him are conscious of betraying as they do it.

Any ambivalence teachers have toward their activity damages their effectiveness in control. The children immediately pick up any sign of hesitation or doubt and use it to their advantage. In contrast to those chronic teachers who believe in the righteousness of their behavior and are therefore taken seriously by the children, the self-conscious acute teachers appear not to uphold what they do. They sabotage their own efforts at control.

The Sense of Unreality

The awareness of many acute teachers that they are participating in an immoral process becomes an everyday fact of life. Often these teachers appear to others in the school as if they were in a daze. They appear only to be going through the motions of being a teacher and come to experience their activity in Midway as unreal. Some of them are even vocal in their contention that they cannot believe what they are doing. Life in Midway becomes a sort of nightmare-horror movie in which they helplessly observe themselves acting.

Certain acute teachers make the discrepancy between their belief and their activity the foundation for a feeling of authenticity in the school. They discuss with like-minded teachers their mutual feeling that what occurs in the school is unreal. They spend hours analyzing the finer points of their dilemma. To some the school and their participation in it appear as an on-going surrealistic play. Two of them spend entire lunch periods sitting on the sofa on the side of the teachers' lunchroom watching, bewildered, the other teachers talk about their cars, stocks, and school affairs.

Once the school appears less than real to these self-conscious teachers, it becomes necessary for them to analyze and dissect the school's workings incessantly in order to keep on "doing a job" and not be overwhelmed by the grim reality. The act of continuous critical analysis is compatible with their participation in what they are analyzing.

The Ambivalent Resistance

Even those teachers who most condemn the policies of the school are quite ambivalent in their condemnation. While they see the school's educational policy as destructive to the children, they accept the notion that successful education is a prerequisite for a "decent job." They feel that the experience in Midway is such torture for the children that there should be some rewards for them at the end. They are aware of the degree to which the parents place their hopes for their children's futures on the school, and the anxiety with which the parents approach their children's educational careers. The teachers conclude that it is their duty to give the children what the parents demand. Of course, the children's resistance to being taught is profound. So, brutality intensifies at the point where the acute teacher seriously attempts to "teach the children something."

When attempts to teach do not bring the desired results, the teacher concludes that the brutality was for nothing. Ultimately it becomes extremely difficult for these self-conscious, guilty teachers to sustain the degree of violence necessary to do the job. Many of them give up serious education and spend most of their energy maintaining minimum control. They depend almost exclusively on praise, bribery, and routines, which, while educationally meaningless, do *involve* the children.

The acute teacher scales down his moral priorities and performance expectations and celebrates what he can accomplish. If he cannot "make it with the children," at least he can control them. If he cannot control them, at least he doesn't manipulate them. If he cannot avoid manipulating them, at least he doesn't brutalize them. The acute teacher then works within a calculus of moral condemnation.

Under normal occupational conditions such a life would be unbearable. But these teachers view their dilemma as a temporary one. They only have to survive until they are twenty-six. Thus, a patchwork survival psychology with all its moral contradictions becomes marginally tolerable. As long as they are not going to be teaching for the rest of their lives, they can view their experience at Midway as a meaningless interlude in their moral biographies. As one teacher concluded, "Sure, I do things here that I don't approve of. But what would I be doing if I were in Vietnam."

Through trial and error the teacher develops an arsenal. The trick is to know when, against whom, and to what degree the weapons are to be used. Some acute teachers are unable to do this. They eventually get fired or quit. One acute teacher left Midway after three weeks, ostensibly having suffered a nervous breakdown. Another acute teacher claimed that one had to "love" and "give to" children. But ultimately she admitted sadly that the only way she could keep some of them quiet was to hit them. She once remarked that she could have "beaten some of them to a pulp." Regardless of how badly she treated them she was unable to give up the idea that they should be treated kindly. Then she began reading a series of books about ghetto schools written by young teachers who had managed to "treat the kids with kindness and teach them something in spite of the system." She expressed her admiration for the authors and her feeling that "this is what it takes." The discrepancy between her ideals and her behavior forced her to leave.

However, most acute teachers are eventually able to lower their standards. Others force them so far from consciousness that their activity in Midway is no longer excessively interfered with. This moral retrenchment and the suppression of consciousness is basic to becoming "chronic." Yelling, grabbing, hitting become "part of the job." Soon, incidents which previously disturbed him leave him unperturbed. Classes getting out of control, children fighting with each other, teachers hitting the children, chaos in the halls and the lunchroom are viewed as part of the everyday life of the school. After a few months one teacher summed it up, "I can take anything." The acute teacher becomes experienced and develops a sardonic sense of humor toward what he can't control.

When Midway's daily life becomes natural and his own participation in it acceptable, the acute teacher has acquired all the crucial elements of chronicity. A level of stability is reached where the teacher becomes confident of his ability to last out his tour of duty in Midway. His ability to control, to detach himself, to "take anything," enhances his prestige and status among his colleagues and superiors, for the very qualities which enable him to survive serve the administrative interest of securing the school and hence improve the security of other teachers. The final step in this process is to elevate the qualities of detachment, impersonality, and self-control into values of Experience, Professionalism, and Dedication, terms generally applied to those teachers thought to be a credit to education. Survival tactics which enable the teacher to be an efficient soldier in Midway's pacification program are now defined as qualities of the ideal educator.

MIDWAY'S TEACHERS erect a variety of defenses against their awareness of a discrepancy between their image of education and the educational tasks they see themselves performing in the school. Chronic teachers involve themselves in the mechanisms of control as a way of making teaching comfortable and demonstrating their competence and superiority over acute teachers. To escape from the immediacy of the present, they ruminate on a better past and anticipate a brighter future in a better school. Acute teachers acquire enough technique to survive marginally in the classroom. They attempt to forget that they are morally corrupted and, if they are unable to do so, maintain that by refusing to engage in some aspect of the school's brutality, they are not corrupted entirely. They look forward to the day when they will no longer be subject to the draft and can resume their moral biographies in their preferred occupations. Irrespective of the type of teacher and the variety and combinations of defenses erected, life in Midway is extremely dissatisfying.

For many teachers life in Midway is a drudgery. Many teachers leave as soon as they can. The school has about a one-hundred per cent turnover every five years. Of the staff of seventy teachers there are only five who have been in

Midway for more than five years. But for many teachers a fast exit is next to impossible. Twenty-five of the acute teachers are avoiding the Vietnam war. All teachers with regular licenses must serve for five years before they can transfer. Long-term chronic teachers must consider the benefits of seniority, the reputations they have acquired, and the administrative jobs they have been given which enable them to maintain distance from the children. Thus, the problem is how to put up with the drudgery for a few more years.

Whatever is desirable about being a teacher at Midway is found in the periods between the required tasks. These periods are located in the teachers' lunchroom, the halls, the general office, the supply rooms, and the restaurants in the immediate vicinity of Midway. When we speak of what teachers do when they need not respond to the pressures of the job and can use time to engage in activities they prefer, we are referring to the counter-world. Though teachers are not aware that they live in a counter-world, they are aware of a complex of opportunities available for their exploitation and the meaning this complex has for them for their survival at Midway. It is our purpose to describe this world, how it is used, and the meaning of its use for Midway's alienated teachers.

Griping

Generally, teachers prefer to talk about the job than do it. They do not like being destroyed, but they clearly enjoy talking about it. Instances of children's irreverence, experienced as a nuisance at best and with personal terror at worst, are described in intricate detail with relish. Completeness of detail and enthusiastic description increase in relation to the distastefulness of the experience.

Those teachers who view themselves as failures and detest what they do, advertise their failure in the teachers' world in exchange for sympathy and attention. A teacher who contributes anecdotal material in the lunchroom and restrooms can be assured of sympathetic attention even from those who might, at other times, condemn the contributor. Speculating on the meaning of these extracurricular conversations one teacher concluded, "Everyone is reminding everyone else that we are all doing the same thing." The suspension of moral judgment and the swapped stories enable the teachers to consider their experience in the school as a collective reality where responsibility for what happens is not personalized or individualized but attributed to the nature of the school itself.

Among certain teachers there is a running competition over who can tell of the greatest failure. A teacher will maintain that he has been subjected to the greatest harassment by children and has been the most totally destroyed. If he claims that his children have been out of their seats, eating candy and food, and leaving the room at will, another with a gleam of superiority in his eyes maintains that *his* children have been doing all of this as well as fighting with each other and throwing books, food, and chairs across the classroom. Another teacher then claims that what the other teachers are talking about happens all the time in his class and that he is used to it. But what really bothers him is when he has to break up three fights at once and face the foul language, books, and chairs directed at *him*. The competitive admission of failure in which the experiences in the classroom are exaggerated and dramatized has the effect of glorifying the job. In dramatizing failure these teachers may shift the emphasis to the impossible conditions under which they must work and the risk and courage involved in doing so.

Likewise in their discussion of experiences with administrators, parents, and the P.T.A., teachers try to outdo each other. Complaints about parents entering the classroom and threatening to get the teacher fired are countered by stories of parents entering the classroom and threatening to beat up the teacher. A teacher claims that he has received the greatest number of "nasty little notes" from an assistant principal in his mailbox. Naturally, another teacher has gotten more. In these contests, the teachers resemble comrades-in-arms trying to reconcile themselves to a decisive defeat.

Sharing failure is one thing; talking about educational values is quite another. Teachers' values may change so rapidly that few of them can be assured of a permanent level of support from anyone. Even with the most intimate confidante, they are careful what they say. What happens is that most teachers end up aping each others' values most of the time. Public conversations between teachers often take on a homogenized quality, a spewing forth of values generally thought to be safe in the teachers' world.

But this homogenization is necessary to the stability of the school as is the suspension of moral judgments. One teacher made the mistake of demanding, in the teachers' lunchroom, that another teacher stop hitting a child. The response of the other teachers present was electric. Everybody turned around quickly to see who was talking. The confronted teacher did not respond and everyone then acted as if they had heard nothing.

Several days later, in a guidance training conference, the offended teacher told indignantly of the other teacher's demand. Everyone in the conference, including several teachers who are privately opposed to hitting children, either supported the accused teacher or sat back and said nothing. In the same conference another teacher told how he had narrowly escaped being assaulted by a mother who thought he was hitting her child. He got immediate sympathy, stories of similar experiences, and jokes about "irrational" parents. At this, another teacher suggested that there were reasons why the parents were so angry, that teachers should "try to understand this and not overreact." Two guidance counselors, a school psychologist, and four other teachers shifted uncomfortably in their chairs. No one commented, and the previous trend of the conversation was resumed. "If teachers don't stand up to the parents when they are attacked for no reason, they will think we are weaklings and will try and get away with anything."

Another teacher went around the school for several weeks offering the eccentric perspective that children's resistance to control was healthy. He hoped someone would agree with him. Teachers cracked back at him, "The children have finally gotten to you." If a teacher attempts to be ideologically genuine and consistent, his views are lightly dismissed.

In spite of their conflicting private views, in public conversations teachers unite in the justification of themselves and the denigration of all those who are not teachers. The denigration of administrators, parents, and children ranges from laughing about and imitating the eccentricities and mannerisms of well-known children and important school figures such as Mrs. Jackson and Dobson to the more direct expressions of anger and hatred. Each teacher has a particular object or scapegoat on whom he focuses his hostility: a child, a parent, an assistant principal, the principal, the district superintendent, or even the superintendent of schools or the mayor. Teachers can then voice their resentment toward the school and their place in it in ways which do not affect their ability to do a job.

Teachers justify themselves with certain rationalizations. Children, parents, and administrators are viewed as making it impossible for them to do a good job. In explaining Midway's failure, teachers refer to the "state of the home," the "state of the family," and the fact that the parents "don't show up" at P.T.A. meetings, open house, and other "parent involvement" events. There is also great concern over "the lack of respect for teachers" that parents are thought to instill in the children. Teachers focus on the threat from Mrs. Jackson and other "militant" parents. Administrators are blamed for their lack of leadership and support and their inability to protect the teachers from the parents, the children, and the district office.

Many teachers begin to label children "stupid," "disruptive," "uneducable." Techniques for disrupting classes, breaking down control, and destroying teachers are not viewed as evidence of intelligence. So, frequently, the disruptive child is called stupid as well. The next step is to say he is an "animal," and so the teacher need not try to educate him—control is all that's necessary.

A teacher can gripe, rationalize, and glorify his failure. But these very activities in their self-justifying nature prevent his making any relevant changes in his job. In effect most of Midway's teachers are convinced that nothing can be done. To the extent that they assume this attitude toward their work and are unable to relieve their anger and anxiety through griping, it becomes important that they pursue activities in the school which they can affirm. Since all of Midway's teachers are dissatisfied with their jobs and griping accomplishes nothing, they cast about for escape routes.

Getting "Time" in the Counter-world

Teachers who depend on the counter-world to affirm their existence in Midway must find ways to increase their access to it. When teachers refer to their counter-world activity they do so by calling attention to their "time." In effect, by "time," teachers mean the time they spend in the counter-world. Each teacher starts with a daily prep period and lunch period which is considered his "time." When a teacher makes statements like "I'm taking my time" or "I'm on my time," she is implying that she need not concern herself with the school and the expectations of administrators and parents. Particularly, "time" implies a legitimate right to maintain distance from children.

Teachers are allowed ten days per year of sick leave with pay. A day absent beyond the ten days allotted means the loss of anywhere from twenty-five to forty dollars. Except for a few Kerner generation people, most teachers use up all their yearly sick leave. Some teachers refuse to be absent more than ten times a year if they can possibly avoid it, but many are not adverse to the indirect purchase of large blocks of time. It is not too high a price to give up a day's pay now and then to escape from their jobs.

A few make a virtue of being absent without pay. They believe they improve their moral standing by suffering financially. At least they aren't there controlling and manipulating the children.

Chronic absenteeism opens up the teacher to criticism from the rest of the staff. When teachers are absent and substitutes cannot be found to replace them, extra teachers called "floaters," and administrative specialists have to take over the regular classes. Regular teachers lose their "time," and control in the school is loosened up dangerously. On days when fifteen to eighteen of the seventy teachers are absent, Midway leans toward chaos.

Children know when there aren't enough teachers around and so take more liberties. Beginning where floaters and substitutes have taken over regular classes, the spirit of rebellion spreads quickly through the school. After a day like this, the extra-harassed teachers take a sharp note of who was absent. It starts to get around that the absent teachers are "unprofessional" and "not doing a job." The teacher who wants to be absent has to weigh the relief against the criticism.

There is one way to be absent and forestall their critics. Since more teachers take their "sick leave" on Mondays and Fridays in order to lengthen their weekend, a teacher who takes "his days" in the middle of the week will probably not adversely affect overall control in the school. However, alienated teachers cannot be absent just as much as they please no matter what days they take. Teachers have been fired for excessive absenteeism.

Most activity geared toward "getting time" takes place within the school. One way is to volunteer for administrative duties which take the teacher away from the classroom. Certain administrative assignments bring with them three or four extra weekly periods away from the children. The degree of autonomy possible in these administrative assignments varies. For example, teachers who distribute and inventory audio-visual aids, science equipment, and art materials are assigned to the supply rooms where the materials are stored. Often the periods allotted for these activities greatly exceed the time needed to do the work. Teachers use the supply rooms as enclaves for escape.

To take another example, those teachers who volunteer for the guidance committee have a weekly period when they meet to discuss guidance groups they run for the children. Coffee and pastry are served often at these conferences. The discussions among the guidance counselor, the school psychologist, and the teachers turn into bull-sessions about the latest goings-on at Midway. Thus with free cake and coffee in a place of relative comfort and seclusion, the volunteer can indulge himself in the activity he so enjoys during his prep and lunch period.

One teacher appreciated the free period, the refreshments, and the talk but disliked the methods and goals of the guidance program. In order to start a guidance group, a teacher must screen the children by having them draw pictures of their families. The pictures are shown to the guidance counselor and the school psychologist and the candidates are selected. The administration refused to grant extra time to teachers to perform this screening, so guidance teachers screened their groups during their prep periods. But the dissenting teacher refused to give up his prep. Administration kept refusing to grant him another period for the screening, and the guidance counselor would not revise the admission procedures. By refusing to give up his time for screening, yet maintaining that he wanted to start a group, he enjoyed the "free" period, discussion, and refreshment for an entire year.

Some administrative duties are more restricting. Teachers who do school accounting have to work in the main office under the eyes of Dobson and the school secretaries. Teachers who have lunchroom and lunchyard duty, run assemblies, and patrol the halls do not even get away from the children. Many teachers in Midway prefer any activity to being in the classroom. Floater teachers are especially relieved when assigned to the gym, the assembly, lunchroom duty, or to Ryley's office. The experience with the children is so threatening that the most menial clerical task which allows them to escape temporarily from the children is appreciated and savored in a manner which people unfamiliar with Midway would not deem appropriate to a college graduate.

Floater teachers, especially, exploit the possibilities of increasing their time. Getting more time is accomplished by cultivating Miss Ryley. Early in the morning Miss Ryley assigns floaters to uncovered classes and gives the regular teachers their preps. She can then assign leftover floaters to cover the lunchroom or assemblies, give them extra preps, or assign them to her office in Room 113. The task of a floater teacher who desires preferential treatment from Miss Ryley is to avoid arguments with her and make himself socially and personally attractive. One floater teacher so successfully pleases Ryley that, whenever she is able to, she gives him extra preps or assigns him to Room 113. During periods of the year when absenteeism is low, he often spends as many as three or four out of the eight periods in a school day in Room 113, stamping books, filing records, and conversing with Miss Ryley.

Many teachers increase their time through favors from other teachers. For instance, a teacher on a prep covers another teacher's class for ten minutes so he can get a cigarette, go to the washroom or to the corner store for a snack. Teachers are usually open to giving up some of their time. By granting these favors they can count on ten minutes' relief in the future when they are under extreme pressure from the children. Some teachers further increase this kind of time by stealing it. They arrive a few minutes late to relieve a teacher or return a few minutes late after having been relieved. Often this kind of theft produces much anger and often the thief is severely berated. "You've got a lot of nerve. That's five minutes of my time." Another teacher griped, "He's breaking my balls." To some teachers, having time stolen, particularly when the victim is under extreme pressure from the children, is grounds for a temper tantrum. The degree of emotion displayed at the loss of time is indicative of the harassed teacher's dependence on it for his stability.

Occasionally a floater teacher is mistakenly assigned to relieve a regular teacher. In the event of such an error the teacher relieved is supposed to report to Room 113 for reassignment. Most teachers don't report, but in sneaking this unexpected time they must avoid being discovered by Ryley. There are places in Midway that are relatively free from administrative surveillance. Ryley rarely visits the teachers' lunchroom. For men the safest place to stay is in the washroom. There are usually a few teachers taking illegitimate time. They can be seen moving cautiously from washroom to supply room, from the teachers' lunchroom to the corner store, and avoiding the halls in the immediate vicinity of Room 113.

Aside from the teachers who are absent a day for a day's pay, a few teachers are known to purchase smaller blocks of time. They purchase preps. The market ranges from $1.50 to $2.50 a prep (forty-five minutes), depending on the demand. Purchasing preps as a way of increasing time is generally frowned upon. It is flagrant evidence of a teacher's lack of dedication, perhaps even of competence. However, *selling* preps is viewed as a legitimate way of making money and serious teachers have been known to sell them. The buyer is degraded; the seller is prouder and richer.

Teachers wait in their classes, glancing at their watches, for lunch periods, preps, opportunities to go to the bathroom, have a cigarette, get a snack, have a card game. There is endless anticipation of upcoming vacations, holidays, and absent days. Days and minutes are counted until the next "time" begins. As the end of "time" approaches, teachers sit in the lunchroom murmuring, "two minutes left . . ."

In bull-sessions during "time," the speculations about the future are rivaled only by the rehashings of the past. Several teachers relive their years in the school with another teacher who is glowing because she has "made it"—she lasted out her five years and got her transfer to a white middle-class school. Another teacher, pregnant, will be "on her time" permanently. But, now, it's back to the drudgery of uncontrolled classes, threatening children, impersonal administrators, and angry parents.

Teachers who feel that their failure approaches bankruptcy look elsewhere for success. At any point they can assess their expertise at getting time against the expertise of other teachers. Once they maximize their time, the only problem is how to use it.

Spending "Time" in the Counter-world

Many acute teachers have images of a future in other occupations about which they speculate with each other. Eight of them are recent graduates of law school and spend much of their free time discussing legal matters, the problems of passing the bar exam, and their attempts to set up part-time legal practices while still teaching. Nine others, but for the Vietnam War, would be accountants, bankers, restaurant owners, and other kinds of businessmen and financiers. The intricacies of accounting, banking, and finance are also discussed with delight by many of the chronic female teachers who are wives and fiancées of businessmen and junior executives.

This financial atmosphere is further enhanced by the large majority of teachers who play the stock market. Throughout Midway, teachers trade tips and talk about the subtleties and intricacies of gambling on the stock exchange.

Teaching provides many women with a monetary base from which their husbands can engage in investments and finance. The job is seen primarily as a source of investment capital. Some male teachers whose wives are also teaching invest their entire bi-monthly paycheck in the stock market. Many teachers, who are as uninvolved in teaching as the job will allow them to be, view it as an opportunity to socialize with other businessmen and sharpen their business acumen. The exchange of tips, claims of business success, and involvement in the risk and uncertainty of finance and gambling lends an air of festivity and excitement to the teachers' world.

Each of the two teachers' lunch periods have a daily poker game. Two to seven teachers participate regularly. Involvement is often so intense that, during the game, many teachers forget they are in a school. A few are terribly disappointed when enough people cannot be found to "get a game going." One teacher will play almost any stakes with only one other person. The daily poker game, more than any other counter-world activity involves a total transformation of the teachers' world.

There are a large number of acute teachers who are also graduate students in history, political science, psychology, and sociology. The teaching jobs are financing their graduate education. Occasionally these students discuss issues related to their fields, but most of the shoptalk is of the pros and cons of various graduate schools, ways of getting through them, and the advantages of college teaching and the "academic life" over teaching at Midway. For these aspiring professors, the experience at Midway dispels whatever hesitancy they might have had about getting the degree.

Teachers heatedly discuss current affairs, international problems, and domestic politics. Many teachers are politically liberal, and there is much talk against the war in Vietnam. Domestic and international crises, riots, assassinations, political careers, and upcoming elections are subjected to endless analysis and speculation. However, in all the political discussions the affirmation of liberal values is divorced from the political issues in the school. Some teachers, who most intensely oppose the war, endorse liberal welfare programs, and identify themselves with liberal political personalities, completely reverse their ground in their activity in the school. They hit the children, attempt to justify it, state that parents are unqualified to run a school, and are opposed to any form of community control. Should another teacher try to show one of these liberals how broad political values relate to concrete issues in the school, he meets immediate resistance. The usual reply is, "I'm tired of talking about the school."

Teachers display to each other the latest in mod clothing, photography equipment, and sportscars and their familiarity with recent hit musicals, films, and entertainment celebrities. Female teachers lightly debate the pros and cons of apartments in various areas of the city, furnishings for them, kitchenware, and the like.

There is usually one party in the making to celebrate a retirement, transfer, marriage, or onset of a school vacation period. Of course, there is a party committee, with one or two aggressive members who collect money from other teachers in the lunchroom, frowning and clucking at those who won't contribute because they can't (or won't) attend. Every now and then a group will decide on the spur of the moment to celebrate something, such as "Thank God it's Friday," and parade off to lunch at one of the "better" restaurants outside the Randolph Park area.

Some male teachers have a remarkable knowledge of the statistics of the major seasonal sports. They discuss matters of averages and percentages long and fervently. Some of these sports bugs (who are usually avid poker players as well) establish and administrate teachers' betting pools on current big-league events. There is usually at least one pool available every school day, and a teacher may find himself solicited twice or more during his lunch period to "throw in a buck." On one World Series day, when a teacher was solicited twice by each of three separate pool-makers, he cracked, "Hey, why don't we have a pool to see who knocks the most heads this week?"

Exploiting opportunities in the counter-world at first provides the teacher some temporary relief. Then, if he gets sympathy, a bit more "time," and maybe wins a baseball pool, he begins to feel that here is an area in his life in the school where he can succeed a little. In fact, he is rather startled at the range of opportunities there are in what he first thought was a very "tight" institution. But his opportunities exist *only* in the loose interstices of the counter-world. In the educational world, no matter what else goes on, the children are controlled. Through socializing, stock tips, abstract politics, teachers subtly validate each other's values, achieve some sense of solidarity, and return to the main business of getting on with the job.

Those teachers who most hate their jobs and who may even have an inkling of Midway's larger purpose can allow themselves to exploit the possibilities of the counter-world with a minimum of guilt. They may come to feel that participation in Midway's underlife is both pleasurable and inconsequential. Certainly they view their underground activity as less grating on their ethics and politics than their image of their relationship to the children. But they are unaware that their relief and pleasure gained in the counter-world allows them to return to the drudgery of teaching refreshed and renewed so that they can bear to do the minimal tasks required for participation in Midway's pacification of its lower-class youth. Thus the counter-world is not only crucial to the teachers' survival but at the same time encourages their illusion of nonparticipation.

Midway school provides its harassed teachers a series of counter-institutions where they can get the satisfaction that the job does not provide. But these avenues of escape and opportunities for self-affirmation in no way hinder the execution of Midway's educational routines. In exchange for the periods in which they can escape from the bureaucracy, pursue their middle-class hobbies, and fantasize about their futures, teachers prepare Midway's youth for lower-class futures in the ghetto.

CHAPTER VII

THE CHILDREN'S ACADEMIC CAREER

MOST TEACHERS are unaware of Midway's significance in the lives of its students. Teachers know that the children live in a "ghetto" and are failing. But most have never ventured beyond the delicatessen two blocks from the school. For them it is nine-to-three, a quick drive out of Randolph Park, or a quick walk to the nearby subway. When inside Midway, they concern themselves with survival. In all their reflections on the state of the school, the difficulty of their jobs, and the failure of the children, Midway's teachers may not realize that the children are learning something that is crucial.

For the children, life in Midway takes on greater significance than whether they are controlled or fail in the narrow sense. Throughout their seven-year career in the school, Midway's Black and Puerto Rican children have extensive contact with white teachers who live outside of Randolph Park. As representatives of the larger society these middle-class commuting teachers, in their contact with Midway's lower-class children, communicate to them the terms of success and failure in white society, and how they are meeting those terms. Through contact with Midway's teachers and administrators, the children learn what the larger society thinks of them and what types of social and economic claims they can make on the larger society. Through Midway School, American society communicates to Randolph Park children what can be expected out of life.

At different stages of their academic career, Midway's children learn the various aspects of a curriculum more relevant to them than the three R's. It is our purpose here to describe this curriculum as it is taught through the stages and the children's response to what they learn.

Kindergarten children are exposed to a wealth of toys, recreational activities, and snacks. The kindergarten room is divided into a number of areas where children can play or not as they please. Thus for most of the three hours they spend in school, the children have the run of the classroom. They can play with blocks, games, and puzzles; they can finger paint, model clay, draw, play house with black and white dolls, work with puppet nurses, doctors, and policemen. Initially, kindergarten appears to the stranger like a logical extension of the home playroom.

The kindergarten teachers are friendly and permissive. They have pleasant, tinkling voices and, like excited and appreciative mothers, instantaneously respond to the children's expressiveness. They rarely scold and never hit the children. Of all the teachers they are the most consistently oriented to the children's values and interests. In class there is much singing and dancing, many games and stories. There are daily cookie and milk snacks and frequent holiday and birthday parties. Kindergarten rooms are decorated according to the season and upcoming holidays. The decorations are supplemented by drawings, cut-outs, and other products of the class. No place in Midway rivals the festiveness and permissiveness of kindergarten.

Floater teachers are pleased when assigned to kindergarten, where they feel they don't have to control the children but can just relax and play with them. If a visitor to Midway spent an entire day in kindergarten early in the school year and took no notice of what was going on in the halls or the lunchroom, he would probably conclude that he was in a progressive school.

However, this atmosphere is slightly misleading, for on the first day the child is taught how, where, and when to hang up his coat, get a drink of water, go to the washroom, get his snack, and perform a variety of other prescribed routines. He is assigned to a table with four or five other children. At various times in between play periods (these are called "work periods" by the teachers), the children are asked to sit at their tables to wait for a snack, listen to a story, watch a movie, or play a game. In the beginning, the ratio of sitting to playing is very low. But as the year progresses, more and more activities are organized in which the children are asked to sit at their tables. By the end of their kindergarten year the children are sitting in their seats most of the time.

Also, there is some curtailment of freedom during the out-of-seat "work periods." The more active children begin their work period by playing with blocks, puppets, or clay in the appropriate area. But they sometimes have difficulty sticking within the boundaries. They often want to use toys in the service of fantasies that intrude on other play areas. For example, children playing with blocks build a fort; then they want to play war and try to use the whole classroom as a battlefield. When playing house, the father, after eating his breakfast of clay on toy dishes, gets a toy car and drives to work via the block area and the finger-painting area. But before he gets to work, he has changed into a race-car driver.

The kindergarten teacher opposes all play fantasies that take the child beyond the approved areas or that use toys for purposes other than those originally intended. Children are told that they must stay in one place at a time. When tinker-toys are made into rocket ships that zoom around the classroom, they are confiscated as is the clay when used for food, the toy cars when they enter other play areas, and the puppets when they leave the puppet stage, for such fantasies are contrary to the school's aim of turning play into work.

The teacher is particularly distressed by the child who tries to transform the entire classroom to fit his fantasies. For such a child is often emulated by the other children. Seeing him using a tinker-toy as an airplane, they all want to join the flight. If not discouraged from his activity, he is often joined by the rest of the children who run around the room, laughing and trampling over the distinctive work areas. In such instances the kindergarten teacher is visibly angry, stops everything, and has the children sit quietly at their seats. The leader is singled out for special punishment, is told to sit in the corner, and receives an individual scolding. If his disruption persists, his mother has to come to school.

All the basics of routinization, control, and punishment begin in kindergarten. The kindergarten experience also lays the groundwork for the chronic deception of the children. To the extent that the child assumes that his career in Midway will be similar to his kindergarten career, he is already being deceived. For all subsequent experience in Midway is characterized by further tightening of controls, constriction of movement, blocking of fantasy, and intensification of punishment when the terms of the school are challenged. In kindergarten the child is seduced into accepting the school. The terms of survival in Midway are not made plain to him.

In first grade, the children discover that they are now expected to be in their seats for most of the six-hour school day. Instead of playing in work areas, having snacks, playing group games, singing songs, and listening to stories, the children now spend the great majority of time reading, writing, and doing arithmetic. While the first-grade teachers remain friendly and do not hit the children, the major emphasis is on routines and academic skills. Very little time is set aside for art, music, and games, and they occupy the lowest place in the teachers' priorities.

For many children the abrupt transition to first grade is experienced as a severe shock. Some are unable to make the transition and withdraw for weeks. Some ask to be sent back to kindergarten, but, of course, they can't be. They then refuse to do any of the academic tasks and may try to leave the room; for these children first grade is a betrayal. Other children do not question the abrupt transition; they approach the new tasks as if they were still in kindergarten.

Many teachers encourage the children to try first grade as a game, to cope with the new restrictions as if they were game rules. They give stars and pats on the head for the correct performance of routines and academic tasks. Some children can cooperate but still miss kindergarten. They plead with the teacher to give them more time to draw, sing, and play. They also lobby for more snacks, drinks of water, and trips to the washroom. The teacher can now withhold art periods and so forth and use them as rewards for cooperation. The majority of the children submit to being routinized in exchange for occasional kindergarten activities.

By second grade the children have been tested and classified according to their reading ability. On that basis they are placed in levels from 2-1 through 2-11, the 2-1 level class being the best readers and the 2-11 the worst. Many of the lower-level teachers can be heard, within earshot of the children, complaining how dumb their classes are and what animals they are, while teachers with upper-level classes boast about the brightness of their children and what a pleasure they are to teach. Relieving a regular teacher, a floater teacher asked, "How are these kids?" "No trouble—they're dumb," came the reply. Only the upper one or two levels are considered bright. So by the second grade four-fifths of the children discover they are "dumb." "Who were you fighting with? How stupid can you be—if you are going to fight with someone at least you should know your opponent's name."

Also, by the second grade most teachers drop any pretense of being accepting parents. Education is no longer defined by teachers as a friendly game, and children begin to resist the pressure of the transition from play to work. Smiles and gentle persuasion are replaced by commands and threats. Corporal punishment is introduced.

Control rapidly becomes the primary issue. Most substitutes and floater teachers and one-third of the regular teachers cannot control their classes. In many of these classes children refuse to do any work, fight with each other, leave the room, run through the halls, and harass the other classrooms.

By the third grade, for many teachers the *only* issue is control. The children are hit, bribed, and manipulated in any way that will secure the class. The children respond by doubling their efforts to defeat the teacher. By the end of the third year, in many classes, education has hardened into open class struggle between teachers and children.

Throughout these years the children are reminded how crucial education is for them. They are informed that now is the time to learn to read and write if they are planning to go to high school or college, and get a decent job. Each teacher promises each new class that he is going to teach them what they have to know. Occasionally a teacher is so effective in control that the children are forced to do some work. But the next year they get a teacher whom they can destroy. Midway's typical child goes through three or four years of defeated teachers.

Regardless of the intensity of the warfare, children are still addressed as if education were happening. The children are not told that they have already failed, only that they are now failing. The cumulative nature of a child's failure is never stated. He is passed to the next grade even though the objective tests given each year show that he is farther and farther behind.

> Dobson: Now I know what is going on in this class. You are not learning anything, and it does not matter how good a teacher you have. If you don't want to learn, no teacher, no matter how hard he tries, can teach you. Now, you're lucky to have a teacher at all. Many classes in the school system are left uncovered because there are not enough teachers; and if we were not on a triple session, you would not have a teacher. But you have a teacher and you are wasting his time and yours, because you spend all your time getting him to bawl you out for not cooperating, rather than let him spend his time teaching you something. Everytime you (he points) and you and you cause him to yell at you and go over to you to correct something disruptive that you are doing, you are wasting your precious time and your classmate's as well as the teacher's time. There are some children who are trying to learn in this class, and everytime you take away the energy of the teacher and use it for correction, that means he can't teach the ones who want to learn. Now, there is no one in this class who is reading up to grade level. In fact, there is not one person in this class who is less than two years behind grade level. Now, if you don't catch up, it will mean that you will never get through high school. You will never get the education you need, and you will never be able to get a good job when you grow up. Now, if you want to catch up, only you can do it. You should be using every precious moment in class doing your work so you can learn to read. You should be reading books outside of class, practicing reading all you can, learning to read not just by reading words, but by trying to understand the meaning of what you read.

The communication of failure increases as control breaks down. In the midst of classroom chaos a teacher may shout, "You can have your fun now, but you'll be sorry in a few years!" A teacher in the process of being destroyed reminds the children that *they* are the ones who are failing.

Many children soon come to habitually negate their own work. The teachers' preoccupation with routines and control leads inevitably to evaluating children's work almost exclusively on its form. Children are rarely rewarded for content. The emphasis is always on neatness in handwriting and arithmetic calculation, clearness in speech, and formulaic answers in social studies and science. Children come to judge their work almost totally in terms of whether or not they have "messed up." A child may spend an entire forty-five minute period doing nothing but heading and reheading his paper, declaring with each reheading, "I messed up." Rejecting everything that isn't perfectly neat "like the book," they succeed in doing nothing. In art class, this preoccupation with tidyness is sadly compulsive. Some children will not allow themselves to finish a drawing because they always "mess up." By adopting these aseptic standards with a vengeance, the children fail themselves more irrevocably than do their teachers.

At the same time the children are being convinced that they are failures, they are urged not to give up. Built into each communication of failure is a corresponding invitation to success. Teachers know that a child who has given up is totally uncontrollable. So, the hope for success must be sustained. The child is always given another chance to succeed on the condition that he conform to the values of the school.

Some teachers succeed temporarily in getting a "disruptive" child interested in some academic activity. They even make vast claims to him about possible future occupational success. Each day they discover budding writers, artists, musicians, mathematicians, and scientists. But these exhortations to perform and invitations to conform have little or no relationship to any possible future success. Children are indiscriminately urged to reform whether they are in the second grade or graduating in a few weeks, whether they are one year below grade level in reading or four years below. By trying to keep alive the children's hope for success *even when they have none,* the teachers hope to avoid the children's rebellion.

Gradually, the children begin to catch on. Graduates of Midway, who attend Porter Junior High School across the park, enter the school late in the day, run wild in the halls, bait the teachers, and innervate the children's rebellion. They are visible evidence of Midway's failure. The children also see their older brothers and sisters dropping out of Porter. Some older brothers and sisters, because they were placed in Midway's high-level classes, have been admitted to better high schools outside Randolph Park where white children also attend. However, in these high schools they are placed in the low-level classes with other Black and Puerto Rican children from other ghettos. The children are subjected to a barrage of evidence that contradicts whatever illusions they might harbor about the worth of their education and the possibility of their future success.

Some perceptive children catch on to the teachers' trick of dangling "success" before their eyes to control them. These children see that, in fact, their failure is cumulative and irreversible; frequently their bitterness shows. In tears, one boy screamed, "You don't care about me! You never taught me nothin'!" The myth that they are being educated is always breaking down.

Midway has a complicated relationship to its children. Under the guise of liberal education calculated to insure the children's upward mobility, Midway assumes the task of both communicating the failure and sustaining the myth of mobility. Thus the school has to maintain a delicate balance between preparing its children for failure and sustaining their hope for success. When the balance is not maintained and the reality of failure overrides the hope for success, the children lose faith in the myth. When the children become aware of the *point-*

lessness of their study, they are forced to reassess the whole school, the teachers, the routines, the bribes, the punishment, and the control. They look for opportunities open to them that may be more profitable than those offered in the educational world.

IN MIDWAY's educational world, the children learn that they are failures. Some, as we have seen, even perceive the absurdity of their whole school career. So it is natural that they seek activities in which they can succeed. Midway provides a series of counter-institutions where children can temper their sense of failure, and which children value as highly as teachers value their counter-world. But the children's counter-world is a tough place. They must learn first to survive in it before it can offer them consolation.

The Violent Reality

While some classes are tightly enough controlled that fights rarely break out, outside the classrooms—in the hallways, the washrooms, the lunchrooms, the school playground, and on the streets and sidewalks in the immediate vicinity of Midway—fights occur regularly. For the children, school is a dangerous place.

Aside from their immediate classroom responsibilities, most teachers feel little or no commitment to protect the children from each other, and the children know it. Many chronic teachers view preventive action with children outside their own

classes as an unnecessary risk. In their refusal to break up
fights in the hallways, they cite the numerous times parents
have complained when they have interceded.

Teachers whose classes are under control often discover to
their dismay that fights break out when they are replaced by
floater teachers. For when regular teachers are absent or on
their preps, all the tensions which have been building up in
the class are expressed. Often an orgy of fighting and destruction follows.

However, in some controlled classes a substitute authority
takes over. If not appointed class president by the teacher,
the strongest child assumes the rule of class dictator on his
own initiative. He patrols the aisles imposing his will, clobbering anyone who is out of line. Occasionally these class
dictators extend their authority to several other classes in their
own grade and several classes below them. But a child whose
strength and aggressiveness insulate him from some disadvantages is open to attack by a bully from a higher grade. Occasionally, to the delight of the rest of the class, the class dictator
is bullied in the same way he bullies them.

Left unprotected by teachers and facing potential violence
on all sides, most children must find ways to protect themselves.

Preoccupation with Defense Alliances

When threatened by other children or teachers, children
brandish the availability of brothers, sisters, cousins, mothers,
fathers, classmates, and friends against their attackers.

Often when a child is in immediate danger of being attacked, he hysterically rattles off the names of the members
of his alliance, how big they are, and what they will do to
his assailant if he is harmed. Often, the size, composition, even
the existence of these alliances is fabricated.

Occasionally children succeed in getting their parents to

defend them against other children. After an extended fight in the schoolyard between two children, the defeated child ran home to tell his mother. The enraged mother charged into the class, told off the child who had beaten up her son and swore that anyone "messing" with her son would have to deal with her. The child replied that she better leave him alone and get out of their class. A series of insults between the parent and the class followed. The parent refused to leave and kept repeating her threats, and the class got more and more enraged. Finally when she was halfway down the hall and walking away from a torrent of jeers and profanity, the parent suddenly stopped, turned around shaking her fists and charged the children. The children charged the parent. The frightened teacher somehow placed himself between the parent and the children, and prevented a clash. He finally convinced the parent to leave. Most children have no adult protection in the school. So when one child does have it, the other children see it as an unfair advantage.

Children take a different attitude toward parental intervention against a teacher. When a parent or older relative takes the trouble to come into Midway to stick up for her children, the children usually back the parent against the teacher. One child, who had been grabbed by her teacher, ran out of the classroom and returned with her older sister. The enraged sister stormed into the class and dressed down the shocked teacher in front of the rest of the children.

> Now you better not touch my sister—you better not lay a hand on her or I'll beat the shit out of you—white man. Judy says that you are crazy—that you are retarded. But you better not lay a hand on her.

At the conclusion of the older sister's tirade, the class applauded and cheered. Since children view teachers as an advantaged opponent whom they cannot effectively combat, it becomes legitimate to enlist the aid of relatives in disputes with them.

Very frightened children depend on fantasy for security in the school. One child's father had disappeared many years ago. Two years ago when he was ten, the child ran away from home to search for him. Once he got so angry at three teachers trying to control him that, after spewing them with four-letter words, he insisted that he was going right home to get his father who would kill them all. He ran out of the school and returned five minutes later with a rock the size of a softball. He stormed up the stairs screaming, "It's okay, I'll do it myself." This is an extreme and sad example of a child's need for adult allies.

Midway's smallest and weakest children often protect themselves through alliances with the class bully. A class bully may choose the weakest child in the class for his special protection. He threatens to beat up the other children if they touch him and lends him comfort when he is attacked. Some children are so small and weak that an attacker would be criticized for hitting them by all the other children. The littlest ones need no allies. All the rest do.

After a fight, members of the defeated child's alliance hug and kiss him and take him to the bathroom where his tears can be dried in privacy. Some teachers, sympathetic to this system of comfort, encourage it. They allow older brothers and sisters to enter the defeated child's classroom, console him, and threaten the victor. Often children will do this in spite of the teacher's opposition. Given the violence, lack of commitment, and coldness of most teachers, the system of alliances must provide comfort as well as protection.

Children are acutely aware that threatening other children, showing off their alliances, and fighting in the presence of the teacher indicate that control has broken down. So children often threaten each other and fight for the purpose of disturbing the teacher's equilibrium. In the middle of such a provocative fight, the combatants smile knowingly at each other. One teacher kept a class after school as punishment. But the class's response was so wild that he had to bar the door with his body to prevent the children from leaving. Two children started a fight in the back of the room. When the teacher interceded everyone else ran out. Children sometimes start fights for more tactically refined objectives.

Alliances are ever-changing and unstable. An alliance which effectively protects a child within his own classroom is usually ineffective in the halls or on the playground. No matter how strong an alliance may be, it doesn't allow most children to feel secure. Many react to the smallest inquiry from another child as if they were about to be attacked. They scream "Get off me!" at a potential opponent even before they are threatened. Some children, when approached by any teacher, duck and cover their heads with their arms. For them, warding off attack is what it means to go to school.

We have dealt above with instances of tactics which children use directly for survival alone. In the remaining areas of the counter-world it will be clear that the children's activities are highly oriented toward survival, but these are also pleasurable activities and can give children a sense of success.

Economic Activity

Throughout the school the children can be seen eating, hiding, exchanging, fighting over, and giving away candy, gum, cookies, cake, potato chips, french fries, soda pop, hero sandwiches, and numerous other foods and sweets. Traffic in food is slightly heavier than traffic in toys, comic books, pornography, sports equipment, weapons, charms, and unidentifiable and unclassifiable objects of value to the children.

The diet of food brought into Midway is fairly stable. But there are fads for certain nonperishables. In one class a child was able to steal a box containing perhaps 1000 thumbtacks.

For the next two weeks, all battles, pranks, tricks, and economic activity between the children was dominated by the thumbtacks. Hoarders hoarded them, entrepreneurs traded them, pranksters put them on other children's seats. Threatened children threatened to throw them. The market had become so flooded with thumbtacks that even when the teacher tightened the surveillance and collected between fifty and one hundred tacks a day, the market was able to sustain itself for about a month.

Consumption and traffic in goods is closely related to the system of alliances. Children make formal transactions for food and nonperishables in exchange for protection from other children. But most economic activity is not so formally or so purely for purposes of hostility. Most children in possession of valued goods willingly share them with their friends. Since the alliances are motivated as much by kinship and friendship as by self-protective considerations, the traffic has an imprecise and almost communitarian quality to it.

Some children distribute their goods as if they were running a business. This is particularly true with nonperishables. The most successful business activity is conducted around the fads. Serious businessmen stock up on whatever they can get hold of. Many children have large stocks of yo-yos, rubber bands, tacks, paper clips, squirt guns, and any other goods which are cyclically in high demand. The problem for the serious child-entrepreneur is to sell at the peak of demand before the fad breaks.

Some children hoard goods purely for their own sake. They often abandon them at the end of the school year. In any one class at the end of the year a few desks can be seen stuffed with artifacts from which could be traced the archeology of the school year from the perspective of the children.

This economic traffic is all the more delightful because it is illegal. In classes that are tightly controlled, many children despair of bringing anything into the classroom. The general rule is for strict teachers to confiscate anything they see and punish the child accordingly. Many children are able to consume and traffic in spite of the embargo. The skills involved in this are subtle and refined. Some children chew gum and swallow food without seeming to move their lips or jaw muscles. Other children hide their possessions so well that the teacher would have to make a thorough search of the child, his desk, and secret hiding places in order to discover them. Shrewd ones intuitively sense when the teacher is going to look their way and instantly hide forbidden objects. Some children are so highly skilled in concealment that even in the most tightly controlled classes they are able to carry on a huge traffic.

The visible use of goods increases in direct proportion to the breakdown in control. In some classes, food, toys, weapons, comic books, and stolen school supplies are displayed on desks and consumed without fear of punishment. The children eat their food with exaggerated gestures and throw their paper airplanes, spin their tops, and squirt their squirt guns in mock dramatic style. The tighter the control in previous classes, the more flagrant their traffic and consumption in uncontrolled classes. By the end of the day the floor resembles the stands of a ballpark after a game. Gum and candy wrappers, cookie crumbs, pieces of smashed hero sandwiches, paper airplanes, rubber bands, and paper clips cover the floor, complementing the usual residue of paper, broken pencils, smashed crayons, torn comic books, and other educational materials.

In classes controlled by class bullies, economic life is highly formal and stylized. A chartable pecking-order develops in which each child knows from whom he can demand food or nonperishables and from whom he cannot. Class bullies often demand goods from their inferiors even in the presence of a teacher. Even if the teacher tells the victim that he doesn't have to give up his possession, the child usually replies that he wants to give it away. The class bullies are expected to protect the weakest children, discipline those children who offend the class codes, and protect the entire class from children in other classes. In exchange for these services, they gain free access to the wealth of the class.

In a few classes, control over economic traffic breaks down so completely and permanently that the teacher comes to accept as natural the freedom the children have won. The unhindered consumption of goods is no longer considered a big deal by the children or the teacher. Where the teacher comes to accept the prerogatives of the children, he still must be on guard against other teachers and administrators less resigned to the children's codes. Interrupted by an enraged administrator, the teacher castigates the children. Since the teacher cannot admit that he allows the freedom, the children bear the brunt of the criticism with tongue in cheek and dutifully hide the nonperishables and stop chewing gum.

However, some teachers draw the line at *visible* consumption. When he discovers a child sneaking a bite of a hero sandwich he has been hiding in his desk, such a teacher remarks with a smile, "C'mon, you can hide it better than that," or "I'll pretend I didn't see it." Discovering a forbidden object, the teacher typically responds: "If I see it again, I'll take it." These teachers demand the form but not the substance of control.

At Halloween, Christmas, and Valentine's Day parties in class, the control on contraband, particularly food, is not only suspended but reversed. Stuffing yourself is the order of the day. For a party, children will spend all their pocket money on candy, soda, and sandwiches, and add these to the teacher's contributions. Then follows a veritable orgy of eating, trading food, sips of soda, stealing bites of sandwiches, and throwing food around the room. Here the consumption approximates the desperate quality of middle-class conventioneers on the loose trying to recapture their youth.

In one teacher's class, control had broken down to the point where children could do almost anything they chose. At a certain point the teacher attempted to reverse the process by starting over with strict routines and the traditional punishments. One child defied the new regime by taking out of his desk a foot-long hero sandwich and chewing on it. The enraged teacher grabbed the sandwich and threw it in the waste basket. The child lost his temper, screamed profanities, knocked over chairs, and threatened to "beat the crap out of" the teacher. The child saw the confiscation of a valued possession, especially food, as nearly a violation of his physical person. His reaction was all the more violent since his hard-won freedom to consume was revoked suddenly.

In a situation where rewards are few and failure imminent, material goods consumed, traded, displayed, and fought over form a tangible basis for self-affirmation in the children's counter-world. However, the sense of well-being derived from consuming and trading in Midway's underworld is less rewarding for most children than some of the more offensive activities they pursue. Unlike the teachers, the children seriously take up the issue of how their time in Midway will be spent.

Teacher Participation in the Children's Counter-world

When administrators, parents, and other teachers are not in view, some teachers at Midway do not attempt to maintain control or to teach the curriculum but play with the children. Whenever possible, they become children themselves.

One floating science teacher turns his lessons into a mock parody of science. By becoming a mad scientist or a magician, he actively teaches the children that science is magic. In class he jokingly casts spells on the children, and threatens to cast a spook on them if they are not good. Other times he dances wildly with the children and shadow-boxes with them. He always does a little Jackie Gleason dance step when entering his classes if the regular teacher has left.

Since he is a floater, all the children know him and call him "giant" and "madman." In the halls he waves at them and chases after them. When he meets them outside the classroom, he shakes their hands. When they call him "monster," he turns into a monster; when they call him "Daddy" and want a hug, he gives them a hug; when they are fighting, he beseeches them to hit him and not each other. In every possible situation, then, he avoids the role of a teacher by taking on the appearance of a clown. By refusing to control the children, refusing to teach, and goofing off with the children he thumbs his nose at the school, the administration, the other teachers, and the parents. In a kind of tacit collusion with the children's counterworld, he relates to children in ways less odious for him than being a Midway teacher.

Sabotage and Counter-attack

Some children attempt to maximize their freedom and avoid authority in the school by spending as much time as possible in the hallways, especially in those hallways where most of the classrooms are empty at the lunch hour. The children Indian-wrestle, play handball, relay-race, and jump rope. Even those teachers whose classes are under control have a few children whom they expel. These children then roam the halls from floor to floor, bathroom to bathroom, baiting volunteer parents on hall duty, and disturbing other classes. Perhaps ten per cent of the children spend one-third to one-half of their school day in the halls.

Becoming a monitor is another way to avoid the classroom. Monitors run errands and do other work for administrators and teachers. After the work or errand is complete, it is expected that the child will roam the halls. A monitor is usually assured of from one to three hours out of the classroom. In principle, "good" children are supposed to be chosen as monitors. But in reality teachers often appoint their worst troublemakers as monitors to get rid of them. Added to the children already there, these troublemakers keep the hallways on the verge of chaos.

One child avoids the school by almost never coming. He plays hooky for as long as two months at a time. When he finally shows up, he doesn't report to class but roams the halls. He baits teachers to chase him around the school and sometimes creates a huge ruckus as two or three teachers try to corner him. When he is finally caught, he sulks in the back of the classroom for a few periods or days, leaves the class, roams the halls for a few more days, and then disappears. He spent about one month of the entire school year in Midway.

Were the children's grievances simple, then the simple sabotage maneuvers mentioned might suffice. But in addition to smouldering with resentment because of their knocked heads, many children begin to see teachers as traitors who invite them to succeed and simultaneously demonstrate their failure. In a sixth-grade class, an angry child demanded, "How come we got these third-grade books?" So children see the teachers as not only the agents of their failure but also as powerful adults who tell them that they are "dumb" and thus deserve to fail.

From the perspective of the child, it is the teacher (not the class and caste structure of American society and the organization of its institutions) who determines his failure. Thus Midway's children who are in the process of failing must do more than sabotage; their response to being betrayed is to rebel. They derive optimum satisfaction in rebellion through destroying the teacher. There is great pleasure in oppressing the oppressor.

While most children attempt to minimize the risk in their rebellion, some children actively seek confrontations with the teacher. Marvin made a point of challenging his teacher to a fight whenever he entered the classroom. When the teacher backed down, he then picked fights with other children as a way of displaying his power over the teacher. After threatening a few children and being told to stop, he usually snapped, "You can't tell me what to do," sat down, read a comic book for a while, left the class for a period or so, and returned to begin anew the cycle of threats. The teacher eventually referred Marvin to the assistant principal, who referred him to the guidance counselor, who referred him to the principal. At each stage of referral, Marvin refused to capitulate and behaved so incorrigibly as to insure referral to a higher authority. After months of conferences and referrals back and forth, the district superintendent was brought in and Marvin was transferred to another school in exchange for a child who was rebelling similarly in that school.

Another child, William, said something mildly derogatory to a teacher, Mr. Koster, who, in turn, approached him and demanded not only that he sit in his seat but that he "face front" and fold his hands. Infuriated at this response, William stood up defiantly and glared. Koster grabbed him and tried to push him into the seat. William struggled out of Koster's grip, stood up straight and made a fist—all the time shouting, "You white motherfucker." Koster kept shouting "Sit down." At that point Morton arrived, assessed the situation, and more quietly told William to sit down. But William put on his cap and attempted to leave the assembly hall. Morton and a young black teacher, Peters, tried to grab him as he walked out but they could barely hold on to him. Morton pleaded with William, "You won't get anywhere if you do anything. Even if it isn't your fault, you'll be blamed." William answered, "Let me be blamed, let me be blamed. Let me at the white motherfucker. I'm going to kill him before the day is out."

For some children, consistent and intense rebellion is their *raison d'être*. Not backing down becomes a point of honor. Also, these blatant and extreme rebels in the vanguard of risk define for other children the degree to which they can safely rebel. The general level of rebellion throughout the school depends on the rebel leaders' successes.

Teachers are targets for rebellion, and so is the physical plant of the school. Children run through the halls, tear down the bulletin board displays, and substitute pornographic displays of their own. During a given day the fire alarm rings ten or fifteen times. In the two new wings, 150 of the windows unprotected by screening were broken. Just about every weekend the school is broken into, windows are smashed, chairs and desks overturned, and books and supplies scattered on the floor. Since the school as well as the teachers are viewed by the children as the agents of oppression and the source of failure, their delight in the destruction of the teacher is further heightened by the destruction of the school.

In the face of their dominant experience in school (in which they are classified, controlled, and told that they are failures), the children set up a counter-world which is meaningful to them. The military alliances, economic activity, sabotage, and counter-attack provide the children with a system of opportunities which they can exploit. At any point in a child's career, he can assess the degree of freedom he has won in class, the emotional state of his teacher, the adequacy of his alliances, his place in the children's economy, and the progress of school destruction. By locating himself in the counter-world and by defining himself according to its values, the child creates a world more relevant for him than routines, lessons, grades, or "points." In the counter-world, children succeed and fail on their own terms.

CHAPTER IX

THE AMBIVALENT
REBELLION

IN PURELY political terms the children's rebellion is surprisingly successful. For the school is often uncontrolled, the hated teachers and administrators are often destroyed, and the children win and hold for themselves interstices of freedom where they can express themselves and affirm each other. But in personal terms the children's rebellion is a more questionable victory. Midway's most successful rebels succeed least clearly.

Except for a few inconsistently supportive teachers, there are no adult models with whom a child can identify in his rebellion. He must sustain it on his own. It is extremely difficult for even the most disillusioned and bitter child to keep up a pure rebellion against the school. In spite of his hostility, he still needs adult praise. But the more he rebels, the more he isolates himself from the source of praise. The more he succeeds in undermining the authority of the school, the more he is labeled by teachers, parents, and administrators as "disruptive," "stupid," "a failure." The more the child succeeds in his rebellion, the more he elicits the adult oppression which previously motivated him to rebel.

The most successful rebel, because of his isolation from adult acceptance, depends totally on other children for support. But eventually he is betrayed by the very children whose own lesser rebellion he makes possible. For the vast majority of children are only part-time rebels and still have ties to adult values. They intermittently sell out for adult acceptance and condemn their rebel leaders. One class was so destructive, the teacher left the school altogether. When a stronger teacher took over, most of the children knuckled under. The rebel leader tried to hold his ground and suddenly found himself being blamed by the other children for all that had gone wrong before and anything that was currently amiss. Further, he discovered himself trapped in the role of scapegoat for the teacher, who made an example of him repeatedly in order to curry favor with the other children and to bring them under control.

Betrayed by the children and used by the teacher, it becomes almost impossible for the serious rebel to go on. Some try to change their ways and rejoin the educational world for periods of a few minutes or hours to several weeks. During these times the child refrains from all disapproved behavior, submits willingly to the routines and may even try to "catch up" by performing some academic tasks. In effect the child attempts to cash in on whatever adult praise may be available to him as a result of his reformation.

When the reformed rebel attempts to meet the school on its own terms, the relieved teacher is often generous with praise and declares that the child will now be successful. Hidden talents and latent potential are suddenly discovered and exaggerated in an attempt to convince the child that he should give up his rebellion permanently. The spectre of possible success in high school and a decent job is once more laid before him.

Some of these converts may be convinced for a while that they are on the road to success. But inevitably, he is betrayed again. Quite soon he discovers that not only are his efforts to reform not taken seriously by the teacher but the teacher has ulterior motives for praising him that have nothing to do with the child's desire for success. Often within earshot of children, teachers tell other teachers how Jack has been controlled by giving him sentences to copy off the board, how Johnny has been told that he is going to be a great scientist and Mary a great writer. The child comes to regard the teacher as contemptuous of his efforts at reform.

Often, however, a reformed rebel reenters the educational world without illusions. The child knows that the teacher is praising him and promising him success totally in the interest of control. In such instances he conforms because he is tired of being an outsider, tired of being criticized, and just wants to be like other children for a while and get some praise. He cannot stand the isolation that rebellion brings.

In a few instances both the teacher and the child are aware of the inauthenticity of each others' actions. Teachers and children go through the ritual of reform and praise with each other, each knowing that the other is putting him on. In such instances cynical smiles accompany the protestations of hidden talent and the promises to be good. In mock dramatic style the teacher and child indulge each other in a game of protestations, each knowing that neither believes in it. The serious rebel then views the game of playing at being a student as a temporary interruption of the serious business of destroying the teacher.

Identification with the Oppressor

There are other dimensions to the children's ambivalence toward their rebellion. Children talk at length about the meanness and strictness of teachers. They enthusiastically describe in specific detail the incidents where they have been most decisively defeated and tightly controlled. This is particularly true when the children have been struck or manhandled by teachers. Many children take obvious delight in recounting to other children and, occasionally teachers, their battle experiences. Having been hit by a teacher with a school-wide reputation for clobbering children is a kind of status symbol. While they resent the power and oppressiveness of teachers, the children at the same time respect and identify with the strength that accompanies oppression.

Children expect teachers to fight for their own interests and are confused and angered when teachers attempt to break or alter the codes of battle. They are particularly angered when teachers attempt to avoid the issue of warfare in the classroom. Many children see classroom conflict as a form of permanent warfare. So the attempt of a teacher to lessen the conflict by offering concessions is viewed as stupid and insane. For the children define the classroom not as a vehicle of education but as a place where teachers and children destroy each other.

The children's identification with strong teachers who control and defeat them is also related to their own situation in the school, in which their survival depends on their ability to protect themselves physically from other children. Self-protection depends on the child's ability to bluff and convince an opponent that it would not be worth it to engage in combat or on his ability to commit himself totally to a fight if there is no other way. In many ways, the mechanisms by which teachers maintain control and protect themselves are similar. Children come to appreciate and identify with a teacher's technical virtuosity apart from the hatred that they harbor toward him as an enemy. The battle involves a professional and technical skill that may be observed and discussed with detachment. At times children appear as involved in recapitulation and dramatization as they are in the on-going fight. An entire folklore is created through which the children can celebrate victories and acknowledge defeats.

However, this warrior pose cannot stand up against the onslaught of the adult world. Lacking adult support for their conception of the school, the children lose confidence in the morality of their rebellion. With the loss of confidence in their position, they conclude that they *should* be defeated—that they are bad and deserve to be threatened, beaten, and humiliated by the teachers. In the face of their oppression children adopt a slave psychology.

They embrace a "higher" morality of goodness and badness which the adult world defines for them and which they have difficulty in shaking off, regardless of their views of the school and its authorities. Almost any teacher, administrator, or parent can get a child to admit that he has been "bad," no matter how bitter he is.

In view of this conflict, some children feel "bad" when they have utterly destroyed a teacher. Some even apologize. Of course, these guilty feelings further aggravate their ambivalence toward their own rebellion, and they are thus more prone to expect and even accept the brutalizing tactics of a strong teacher.

Given the institutional realities of Midway School, the children find themselves in a series of dilemmas. They are subjected to a tightly formalized and routinized existence which gives them very little return. Faced with this restricting and unrewarding educational career, the children fall back on and cultivate their own world with its own system of opportunities which is separate from the world of education, which they greatly prefer to it, and which they attempt to impose on the rhythm of the school. But the school sees all these "childish" activities as illegitimate. The rejection of any child by the adult world intensifies in direct relationship to his tactical success. Those who do rebel are forced to partially reject their own rebellion and identify with their adult oppressors. Despite their impression that they are betrayed, exploited, and brutalized by the school, the children are unable to rebel without ambivalence, loss of self-confidence, moral guilt, and fear of adult disapproval and punishment. The more the children rebel, the more they eventually accept their status as unworthy failures, given them by Midway's adults.

Most of Midway's children fluctuate between the educational and the counter-world, attempting to reap the benefits of both. At the point where opportunities in the counter-world appear to be blocked by a strong teacher, children return to the educational world seeking praise and hoping for success. At the point where control breaks down or disillusion predominates, the children return to the world of underground activity, sabotage, and rebellion. The adult world holds forth the promise of acceptance and success only to be revealed as the source of the communication of failure. The counter-world offers immediate gratification on the children's terms but isolates the children from adult acceptance and any hope for eventual success. By attempting to live in both worlds, the children realize little benefit from either.

But this patchwork style that most of Midway's children pursue is not without educational consequence. For the style of consumption, noncooperation, and rebellion followed by submissive cooperation in exchange for crumbs is perfectly consistent with the quality of life the children will lead when they graduate from Midway, drop out of Porter Junior High School, go on welfare, and obtain the lowest-level jobs. The skills learned by the children in their counter-world of subterfuge, sabotage, and free-wheeling underground economic activity will be highly utilitarian in their adult life in a ghetto. Especially useful are the skills in manipulating or kow-towing to authority, for many ghetto citizens spend considerable time negotiating with public assistance centers, hospitals, free clinics, police agencies, and other welfare and lower-level job bureaucracies. The school familiarizes its students with the terms of survival in the ghetto and inculcates a psychology of acceptance of lower-class existence. In educating for lower-class ghetto life, Midway school is exceptionally successful.

CHAPTER X

MIDWAY SCHOOL is a world of harassed teachers, angry parents and disillusioned children. It is a chaotic, often brutal world in which teachers and children destroy each other. The chief characteristic of the administration is that it lacks the ability to control the situation. In the face of this chaos it attempts at best to impose a countervailing administrative reality. So that for everything that occurs in Midway, there are two coexisting interpretive and descriptive languages—the emotional outbursts of parents, teachers, and children and the bland professional language of administration. It is our concern here to describe this administrative world, its effect on the school, and the attempts of its carriers, Dobson, Morton, and Ryley, to mediate between the conflicting demands of their administrative superiors, parents, and teachers.

The Principal and the Higher Administrative Echelons

To his administrative superiors in the central office of the Board of Education and the district office, Mr. Dobson has to comply with a complex network of legalistic and bureaucratic directives. The directives cover everything: what curriculum should be taught and in what manner; when, and in what way teachers and children should be dealt with in cases of infractions; how parents should be treated and how teachers and children should feel. Often Dobson reads or paraphrases directives from the higher offices to children over the loud speaker in each classroom. He also does this to teachers in staff conferences and training sessions. However, most of the directives are communicated through the hundreds of circulars distributed to the teachers each year. The circulars describe the techniques and procedures for everything: minutes allotted per week per curriculum area, how to teach lessons, write lesson plans, decorate the classrooms and hall bulletin boards, set up routines and control classes, send children through the halls, conduct fire and air raid drills, order supplies, use "audio-visual aids," refer "problem children" to reading and hearing specialists and "disruptive" children to the guidance counselor for "guidance" or "suspension." In their total effect, the circulars attempt to delineate how teachers should act in all possible situations.

All these rules, procedures, techniques, and priorities comprise a system which, if it operated ideally, would leave nothing that occurred in the school to chance. Midway would operate like a machine.

Of course, Midway does not operate according to the model described in the circulars; and Dobson's crucial problem with the higher administrators is that he has to appear as if he and the school were responding to their directives. One way of appearing to do so is to pass the directives down to the teachers. While Dobson is aware that most of the directives are not followed and many are not even read, at least he can claim that he has passed them down and thus cover himself with his superiors.

But the higher administrative echelons also want evidence that the directives are being applied. Dobson satisfies this demand by presenting statistical data that so many children are being taught so many subjects on such and such a level by a qualified specialist in accordance with rules and procedures described in the circulars. At the same time he attempts to keep any information about what is actually going on in Midway from filtering up to his superiors. They do not want to learn what is going on, because direct knowledge of the school involves them on a personal level. This is distasteful to them. Thus Dobson's central task is to maintain distance between Midway and higher administrative echelons.

The major task of the higher offices is to compile statistical evidence that Midway and other schools in District 7 are complying with the directives. So that when politicians, civil rights groups, community-control advocates, and journalists attempt to expose Midway, the higher offices will have a mass of evidence showing that "the school has done its best," that a "rational educational process has been going on," that "directives against corporal punishment" have been issued, and that "new and innovative programs are being tried in depth."

The statistical evidence is also used to justify claims on the federal and state budgets. Among the highest priorities in Midway is the taking of attendance. Careful attendance records have to be kept, not only to cover the school with the courts but to document the legitimacy of the dollar-and-a-half the Board of Education receives from the state per child per day. Inexperienced teachers are continually reminded, "If you do nothing else, take attendance properly." Those secretaries responsible for pooling attendance records and other information behave toward teachers as if collecting data were the school's only task and the teacher's only duty.

It is expected by his superiors that Dobson will insulate them from any situations in Midway which could be used as a basis for attacking the district and central office. Whenever an administrative superior is made vulnerable to attack by a situation in Midway, he attempts to redirect the responsibility for the situation back to Dobson. Stratton, the District Superintendent, attempted to fire a teacher (Rosen) who had been accused of hitting a child. The angry teachers called a meeting with Stratton.

Stratton: Have you invited Dobson?
Teacher: No, for our purposes, we didn't think it was necessary.
Stratton: I think it is discourteous not to invite the principal of the school if you are going to discuss him or anything about the school. After all, he is responsible for the school and if you are going to be discussing his school, he should be confronted directly, shouldn't he?

In the discussion that followed, the teachers tried to communicate to Stratton that it was *he* they wanted to confront and not Dobson. Dobson had no say in the attempt to fire Rosen or in the final decision to transfer him.

Stratton: I think I am going to have to leave this meeting because you are violating one of the basic ground rules. I say it is unprofessional and unethical for me to sit with a committee to discuss a school for which Mr. Dobson is responsible under the By-laws.

The teachers finally agreed to have Dobson attend the meeting. During the meeting, Stratton pressed the point that since Dobson was responsible for what happened in the school, all the complaints should be directed to Dobson and not to him. The teachers, who viewed Dobson as Stratton's "patsy" and "errand boy," wanted to press their attack on Stratton. But Stratton insisted on chairing the meeting, then revised the agenda, set an hour-and-a-half time limit, and talked ninety per cent of the time. When some of the teachers attempted to confront him with the fact that he, not Dobson had transferred Rosen, Stratton became emotional. "The case is closed. I won't talk about it any more. If you insist on attacking me in this indiscriminate way, I will have to leave." Stratton used all his official advantages and administrative skills to keep from being attacked. In this way, he controlled the school without being held responsible for the effects of his decisions.

Only when he informs the higher echelons of the smooth running of Midway and keeps other communications to a minimum can Dobson feel that he is doing an acceptable job in the eyes of his superiors. But when Dodson is unable to prevent information that tarnishes Midway's public image from getting out of the school, these superiors view it as evidence that Dobson is not controlling his school. Also, when his superiors make an unpopular decision over which he has no control, they pass the buck back to him. Thus, the more routine and normalized his communication with his superiors becomes, the more he can feel that he is doing his job.

The Administration and the Teachers

As a public figure in Midway, Dobson is seen by teachers as a caricature of the very directives he is supposed to implement. Most of his public pronouncements reflect the style and line of his administrative superiors to such an extent that it is difficult to tell whether he is reading a handed-down directive or one he has written himself. Once, the teachers returned to Midway from summer vacation the Friday before the onset of a teachers' strike. Dobson, knowing that no one would show up for work the following Monday, welcomed back the staff in all seriousness and expressed the hope that when school opened the following Monday it would be the beginning of a very successful teaching year for all of them.

At the beginning of each school year Dobson addresses the new teachers and tells them that their first year at Midway School will be "the hardest job they have ever or will ever have," that if they "make it through the first year, no matter how impossible it seems, the next year will be easier."

Throughout the year, whenever a newly destroyed tearful teacher comes into the principal's office, he repeats what he said at the beginning of the year. When emergencies occur that are not covered by the rules or that do not seem applicable to any of the known options, he picks out a stock response that seems to him to fit the situation.

This formulaic approach also characterizes the relationships of assistant principals to teachers. For example, whenever an inexperienced teacher is having difficulty controlling a child, the assistant principal tells the teacher to "take an anecdotal record," "send a letter home to his parents," "call his mother in," or "threaten to have him suspended." There is a variety of recipes that the administration has for the solution of the teachers' problems.

There is a prescribed series of steps to be taken by a teacher before any problem can be legitimately referred elsewhere, so an administrator can put off a teacher indefinitely by holding him to the letter of the protocol. An administrator who uses protocol as a way of protecting himself from Midway's problems need not anger the teachers. Though aware that they are being simply put off in a socially acceptable way, most teachers prefer "Have you been keeping an anecdotal record?" or, "Did you send a letter home?" to a "Don't bother me. I have enough problems," or "Go away. I'm not here." Thus, a tactful administrator who knows his options well enough and uses them skillfully can protect himself from the teachers' problems without appearing to do so.

Occasionally Dobson attempts to communicate with his teachers; but whenever he responds to the needs of teachers on their terms, he comes into conflict with the district office. For example, Stratton directed Dobson to call a teachers' meeting to discuss the P.T.A.'s grievances. Dobson began the meeting by reading the teachers some excerpts of a position paper written by Stratton which stressed that the community was "demanding a say in the school system" and that the

"Carter Report,"* or something like it, was going to be instituted in District 7, and that "we better be ready for it." Dobson then read Stratton's list of the parents' grievances that indicated their dissatisfaction with the "thirty inexperienced teachers," "their poor attitude toward their job," their "smoking in the halls," the "sloppy appearance of some of them," the "long rest periods" that they give the children, and the fact that they do not "teach the curriculum." After reading the grievances Dobson added that Stratton had asked him to "feel free to terminate the services of any teacher who is not doing his job." He closed with the comment, "And Stratton said to me, 'Look, don't hesitate to fire anybody. If these people aren't doing their job, we can't do worse by getting someone else!'"

The angry teachers replied that "supervisors should back their teachers instead of criticizing them," that the children were "rough to handle," and that the inexperienced teachers were being "harassed" by Stratton and nothing was being done about it. One teacher summed it up: "After all, we are adults with a college education. This is not a military operation."

Faced with this counter-attack, Dobson abruptly changed his line. He agreed that "administration should support its staff," and indicated that he disagreed with Mr. Stratton about certain things, particularly about the way Stratton gave credence to Mrs. Jackson's complaints. He went so far as to state that Mrs. Jackson "should be discredited" and "told off by the community." He said that many times he had almost thought of retiring because of his disagreements with Stratton and the parents. He went on:

The schools are a scapegoat, are being used as a scapegoat and will continue to be used as a scapegoat until society

---

*A plan for decentralizing school control in cities.

recognizes its responsibilities. It's almost an impossible situation, almost hopeless, but we should not give up.

Immediately after Dobson finished, Stratton unexpectedly joined the meeting. He stated that obviously "communication had broken down between the school and the community," reiterated the previous criticisms that he had given Dobson to give the teachers, and closed the meeting with the observation that it was "good to see the staff at Midway School getting together with each other to iron out the communication problems with the parents." Dobson's response to this was to stand next to Stratton and nod his head in agreement with everything he said. Dobson had publicly changed his line twice in fifteen minutes.

In spite of Dobson's once having been a teacher himself, it is nearly impossible for him to sustain a style congenial to teachers. The more he attempts to operate on their terms, the deeper his conflict with Stratton and the parents.

While the teachers see Dobson as a patsy and a double-dealer, he sees them as incompetent. Their incompetence springs from their combined lack of experience, professionalism, and dedication. They do not read and follow the circulars. Many have not yet learned how to control their classes. Many are thought not to care. They do not take their jobs seriously, refuse to carry out administrative assignments such as decorating bulletin boards and handing in clerical work on time, are often late, and are absent as much as possible. They do not plan their lessons. In effect they do not work for the children. With so many inexperienced, uncommitted teachers it is impossible to raise reading scores and complete other tasks crucial to academic success.

Morton, on the other hand, does not have such a one-sided view of teachers and often goes to great lengths to cultivate relationships with them. He is thought to have an understanding of their problems and he projects a genuine sympathy for their difficulties. He has also been known to show an awareness of the absurd and ludicrous position that teachers feel themselves to be in at Midway, and to indulge in a kind of self-deprecating humor not normally expected from a serious administrator.

When Morton urges inexperienced teachers not to take difficulties with the children personally, not to get involved with them, and not to lose their tempers, the teachers sense he is speaking from personal experience. And when they see him losing his temper and acting like an inexperienced teacher with children, they can readily identify with him: he exhibits none of the chronic teacher's pretensions toward "tightness." He has even expressed a desire to join in the daily card game in the teachers' lunchroom. In many ways he is "almost one of the boys."

But there is another side to Morton that causes some teachers to discuss him endlessly, trying to figure out "what really makes him tick." Morton is a stickler for rules, lesson plans, and other administrative deadlines. Many of his public pronouncements are similar to Dobson's. But unlike Dobson, he expects the directives to be followed and takes it personally when they are not. Many teachers are convinced that Morton believes that if somehow all the circulars were read, everybody followed the rules, and everybody spent a lot of time planning their lessons, the problems of Midway would be solved. So that when teachers stop working on Morton's terms, he drops the informality, sends them letters, and takes on the style of Dobson.

A sixth-grade class was totally out of control. The children had literally taken it over, and they assaulted the teacher both verbally and physically. But the relationship between this teacher and Morton had deteriorated to the point where the teacher never asked Morton for anything; Morton never spoke to him and avoided his class. The chaotic situation was allowed to continue for a year. Morton's total refusal to work with an inexperienced teacher who was having problems resulted in the isolation of the teacher and his class from the rest of the school.

But for those teachers whose work especially satisfies Morton, permissiveness reaches the comical dimension. One afternoon in Midway's lunchroom, a new teacher, who had been doing a "tremendous job" from the viewpoint of the administration, took a cap gun from a child and fired it several times. Morton, who happened to be in the lunchroom, turned around with a pained expression on his face. When he realized it was his favored teacher who had fired the cap gun, his facial expression immediately changed to a smile. He then pretended as if he had been hit by the shot and feigned a cowboy death scene.

In effect, Morton's style with the teachers, fluctuating between a self-deprecating openness that they find attractive and an unbending formality that repulses them, is only a variation on the general administrative tone. Like Dobson, Morton is unable to consistently communicate with teachers, and, like Dobson, he is aware of his failure to administrate a successful educational program.

Seeing the situation in this light, Midway's administrators give up the educational vision and lapse into a garrison mentality. The school is viewed as a fortress in which each area is vulnerable to attack by uncontrolled children. The administrators come to see their job as securing the fortress, and their immediate task is to see that all classes are covered and other areas of the school such as the halls, the lunchrooms, and the assembly hall are secured. Securing the school involves the judicious placing and use of available teachers, aides,* and volunteers. Their task is complicated by the average daily absence of seven teachers. There are seldom enough teachers to secure the school.

---

*Persons hired from the community to help out with control and administrative jobs.

Miss Ryley, who is responsible for the daily placement of teachers, spends the first few hours of each school day assigning floater teachers and substitutes to classes left uncovered by absent regular teachers. When this is finished, any leftover floaters are assigned to classes in order to give "prep" periods to the regular teachers. School aides and volunteers are then assigned to guard the halls. A very "strong" teacher is assigned to the lunchroom.

Accomplishing this task is crucial not only to the stability of the school and the comfort of its teachers, but also to the administrators. When control breaks down and the preps are not given, teachers put pressure on administrators by complaining about their lack of preps and by sending "disruptive" children down to the administrative offices. Administrators are also called to classes that are totally out of control. A breakdown in control forces administrators into direct contact with the children and makes them vulnerable to attack by the parents who see evidence that the administration is not controlling the school.

The high priority that administration comes to place on control narrows their view of teachers. Teachers are evaluated by administrators almost exclusively in terms of their proficiency in control. (As one teacher said, "Things are *professional* when you agree with the policy of the administration; they are *unprofessional* when you don't.") This proficiency ranges from those who can effectively handle any class or extra-curricular assignment to those for whom even the easiest assignment entails a certain risk.

Miss Ryley accumulates information about teachers' ability to control specific classes. Occasionally teachers who have low ratings in the control of most classes are able to control a class that more proficient teachers cannot. While Miss Ryley has the final decision as to which floaters and which substitutes are assigned to which classes, there is much maneuvering for preferred assignments. At the beginning of a school day,

Ryley's office takes on the atmosphere of an auction. Teachers bid and bargain for preferred classes and attempt to avoid others. Much of this is tolerated by Ryley because it is crucial to her collection of intelligence. If at all possible, she accedes to a teacher's protest about an assignment to a class he abhors or fears. Occasionally she assigns teachers who have angered her to classes that they are having difficulty with. But in doing so, Ryley always has to weigh her desire for revenge against the possibility that the class may get completely out of control and force her into an unnecessary contact with the children.

She seems happiest when she has an excess of teachers and can free some of them from the classroom to file records, open crates of new books and stamp them, make inventories of stored supplies, and run errands for her. When freed from the demands of teachers and children, she jokes with teachers about giving extra preps or taking them away, taking a day off, or about especially disruptive children or classes. But when she is asked for a prep which she feels is unjustified, is blamed for not fulfilling her supervisory role, or is under pressure from children or teachers, she reacts with cutting ferocity. She screams at teachers the way teachers scream at the children. When called into her office, teachers never know what to expect. Through her judicious use of ferocity, Miss Ryley protects herself from excessive demands.

Breakdown in control increases in proportion to the number of teachers who are absent on a given day and the lack of substitutes. Since Midway is considered a "rough" school, substitutes are difficult to obtain. Even with all the calculation in the placement of teachers and bargaining for preferred assignments, the administration only rarely secures the school completely.

The administration is then faced with the problem of avoiding uncontrolled children. Harassed teachers put pressure on administrators by sending "disruptive" children to their offices. The administrators retaliate by sending the child back to the classroom and reminding the teacher that it is his responsibility to maintain discipline. The teacher sends the child back to the office and reminds the administrator that if a "disruptive" child is making it impossible for him to teach, he can demand that the child be removed from class. In Midway, children are often shuffled back and forth between the office and the classroom in a war of nerves between administrators and teachers.

But when the pressure from children is too intense or teachers are too aggressive in asserting their rights to relief, the administrators retaliate through their channels of reprimand. If a teacher fails to hand in clerical work or complete other administrative tasks on time, is late for work, or takes five minutes extra for lunch, the administrator can send him a letter of reprimand, have him sign it, and put it in his permanent file. As teachers' pressure on administration increases, so do the letters of reprimand.

At one point, a committee of five was chosen to represent the teachers in meetings with administration to discuss grievances and "ways of improving the school." During two meetings administrators and teachers blamed each other for the state of the school. After the second one, letters about lateness and incomplete clerical work appeared in the committee members' mailboxes. In many instances those teachers who received letters were generally acknowledged to be among the most effective and dedicated in the school. The barrage of letters had the immediate effect of silencing the attack on administration. Only one more sparsely attended meeting was held.

However, the use of mass reprisals is an extreme tactic that administration would like to avoid. As long as teachers appear to have a certain amount of understanding of the administrations' problems and empathy with their difficulties, do not attempt to hold them to all their formal responsibilities as administrators, and do not blame them for the state of the school, administrators overlook a certain number of infractions. In exchange for exemption from moral responsibility for the school, the administrators exempt teachers from a few legalistic and clerical chores.

Though administrators and teachers would like to publicly expose one anothers' irresponsibility, mutual security dictates a more conciliatory relationship. When things are going smoothly between teachers and administrators, they affirm each other by criticizing children and parents, acknowledging their common difficulties with them. Through the repeated denigration of children and parents, the teachers and administrators attempt to convince each other that they are friends rather than enemies. But this compulsive and ritualistic denigration of the enemy only thinly masks their mutual ambivalence and distrust.

A teacher is having difficulty with a class and is forced to call in an administrator. The administrator bawls out the children and makes an aside joke to the teacher as a gesture of sympathy, but the teacher senses that the sympathy is contrived. He feels that the administrator despises him for his incompetence, just as he, while feigning appreciation for the intervention, despises the administrator for what he imagines the administrator thinks of him. The teacher may be sincerely grateful for the relief and may even imitate the style of the administrator when he has left, but the antagonism lingers for both parties.

Administration senses the lack of respect from teachers. Even when the circulars are read, are followed, assignments are done, and appreciation is expressed, administrators sense the underlying animosity. Dobson's response is to withdraw further into administrative details and spend more time in his office and less with the teachers.

Teachers look to administration for moral leadership. They are handed recipes for achieving control. Many dislike these formulas but use them because they work. They do not reject the administrative techniques, for they are unable to develop ethically acceptable alternative ways of relating to children. They then resent the administrators for setting the tone of their relationship to the children.

The Administration and the Parents

As Midway's principal, Dobson is the most accountable to the parents. He is the most visible and available symbol on whom parents can focus their frustrations and hostility when they feel that the school is failing their children. Parents are permanently dissatisfied with Midway, for they accept the school's terms of success for their children. They take the objective scores on reading tests at face value. They also accept the notion that before the children can learn they must be controlled. When they learn of their children's low reading and math scores and see them running around in the halls and taking over the classrooms, the parents conclude that the school is not doing its job.

The parents affirm a caricature of middle-class education. They would like to see their children controlled to the point where challenging the authority of the school would be unthinkable. The school would operate like a well-oiled machine engaged in the production of marketably educated children.

The parents want basic reading, writing, and arithmetic skills stressed and music and art deemphasized. They are aware that their children are behind in basic skills and that the reading test scores are the major indications of future academic success or failure. Every minute in the classroom should be used to further the chances of their children getting through the educational system with its accrued occupational rewards at the end. Anything which cannot be seen as directly furthering this end is viewed as a waste of time.

The nature of parental expectations exacerbates their relations with administration. The parents want immediate results and the administration has failed them. The parents charge Dobson with this failure; for, from the standpoint of parents, it is not the "nature of the community" or the "state of the home" which is responsible for the lack of results, but the policies of the school and the quality of its teachers and administrators.

Parents are somewhat aware of the real difficulty in educating their children. And they might be willing to overlook some of Midway's shortcomings if its principal would only communicate with them. Lacking immediate satisfaction they might settle for an honest statement of the problem from Dobson. Because of his chronically passive relationship to his superiors, Dobson is incapable of the type of diagnosis that would be acceptable to parents.

He tries to handle all complaints from parents rationally. A parent tells him the books are inadequate and the teachers incompetent. To a complaint about books, Dobson asks which books and which classes they are used for. The parent specifies the books, and says that they are no good because her children can't understand them. Dobson replies with the formula, "These books are being used throughout the school system." If this is not feasible, he admits that the books are inadequate but that the school doesn't have sufficient funds to order new books. To a complaint about the incompetence of a teacher, Dobson asks the parent where she got her information. If she got it from her child, he discredits the child's complaint with the statement, "Children sometimes make up stories about their teachers." If this does not satisfy the parent, and the teacher is new, Dobson maintains that he is an "inexperienced teacher" and that the school will soon be offering him an in-service training course so that he can become more effective. While Dobson demands maximum specificity in parents' complaints, he is as evasive as possible in his replies.

Teachers usually ask children to write a composition about "what I did this summer" on their first day back to school.

Parents are suspicious of the educational value of this practice. Children groan when this is asked of them year after year. When an angry parent questioned this policy, Dobson got up and gave a long speech explaining how the writing of the paragraph involved "oral communication," "writing and composition," "sentence structure," "phonics," "spelling and grammar." He further stated that writing the paragraph about the summer vacation interrelated and combined all of the skills needed in "language arts." "It's not what happened during the summer that's important, but all the activities involved in *communicating* what was done during the summer." Dobson redefines the parent's complaint and answers as if he had been asked about pedagogic ideology.

By rationalizing and redefining all complaints in ways that no longer indict the school and its staff, the complaints lose their critical relevance. By redefining the nature of the complaint and the basis upon which it can be legitimately rectified, Dobson has a self-exonerating answer for anything that occurs in the school. He need not come to terms with parents' feelings about Midway.

The parents are not satisfied. They are convinced that Dobson is devious and evasive, that he is concerned with his own survival, and that he doesn't care about the children. The more Dobson tries to talk his way out of responsibility for the state of the school, the more the parents hold him responsible for its state.

Dobson's problem with parents comes to focus in his relationship with the P.T.A. The P.T.A. has about fifteen active members and for the past two years has been dominated by its president, Mrs. Jackson. Jackson is extremely critical toward teachers and administrators. She says that many teachers are not interested in the children but are just in the school to "collect a paycheck" and "avoid the draft."

I know why there are so many white men here. They aren't interested in teaching. . . . Vietnam!"

Mrs. Jackson's attack is best illustrated in the monthly P.T.A. meeting. She begins the meeting by asking everyone to stand and recite the twenty-third Psalm. After the prayer, she speaks:

I want to welcome you all to this Parent-Teachers' Association. Now it's very important that we all of us parents unite and work together so we can get the education that we want for our children. We know our children are behind. They're getting dumber and dumber every day. We know that their education is at stake and without education—it comes out in the paycheck, and without the education you can't get a decent job. (Applause and shouts of approval from the audience.) Now we were united last year and we fought hard and I think, I hope, we got something done. I think, I hope, all our children got the books. Now I say we fought hard last year and this year we got to stay united, and if we do—if we stick together—we can get anything we want for our children. It's up to us. It does my heart a good turn to see all these other schools with parents getting together for things they want, and we can do it, too. So spread the word and let's get to work. What we got to have is a parent checking on the teachers in each class and reporting to me. When they don't teach right, I can take it up with Mr. Dobson.

Mrs. Jackson then responds to questions and statements from other parents.

Parent: Well, what's the use of the children bringing home the book if, well, they bring them home every night but don't read them. The teachers don't make homework assignments in them.

Another Parent: Not only that, but we know how far behind our children are in reading—usually two years, and so what good is it if you have a fifth-grade book in social studies and the child can only read in the third grade. My son said to me he didn't even like the book.

Jackson: Well, I'm glad you brought that up because it

shows what kind of teachers we got, some of them, and what we got to do; and give me the class of your child. I'm going to bring this up to Mr. Dobson. I'll face him first thing tomorrow and he better get his teachers on the ball. Now he says half of them are very young. They are inexperienced and we can't expect them to teach so good, so the books will have to do it. They just have to assign homework in the books. Well, he better, or they shouldn't be teaching—getting paid for doing nothing. Now, I don't expect the teachers to love our children, but they better teach and we're going to have parents and the children checking on every teacher to see she does her job if she is going to be paid and go on strike and our children miss three weeks of school and all those holidays. I tell you the only way we are gonna get anything is if we fight for it. So now let me write that down and I'll face Mr. Dobson tomorrow and Mr. Morton and Miss Ryley better get down on those young teachers. There's other things I know. I know the teachers aren't teaching and I'm not going to bring it up here but when I face Mr. Dobson and if I don't get satisfaction from him I go to Mr. Stratton. The teachers they got the TV on from 9 to 10:30 in the morning. I find out these things and I'm going to face him with it.

Dobson's public response to Jackson's attacks varies with his audience. In direct encounters with Jackson he is typically formal, but his logical explanations infuriate her even more. Her verbal attacks on Dobson intensify in relation to the "reasonableness" of his response.

With new teachers just assigned to Midway, Dobson understates the problem:

About our P.T.A., we have a very inactive P.T.A. One woman who is president of the P.T.A. is articulate. She is not really articulate because I can't always understand her. Well, she makes her demands fairly well known. Her ideas don't always go along with ours. P.T.A. meets the second Wednesday of every month. There is an average of fifteen to thirty parents. What happens is that this woman does most of the talking and the rest of the parents listen. There may be more activity this year because we have gotten a few parents who really seem interested in doing something and just don't want to sit and listen.

In his joint appearances with Stratton, he talks to the teachers about the need to "absorb" or "neutralize" Mrs. Jackson. They hope to do this by "better communication" and by eventually bringing parents into the P.T.A. who are more compatible with the ideas of administration.

But with the more experienced teachers, Dobson is more candid in his image of Jackson. He has remarked that he feels that Jackson should be "discredited" and "told off by the community." He senses that Jackson is more feared and respected than he is. Furthermore, he is aware that the teachers are convinced that "Jackson runs the school." In private he has admitted to certain teachers that the "parents are becoming the supervisors."

Dobson's inability to respond to the parents on their terms compounds his difficulties with them. His inability to protect the teachers from Jackson aggravates his relations with the teachers. When he attempts to protect the school and the teachers from the parents, he infuriates the parents. When he gives any credence to the complaints of the parents he infuriates his teachers. When he attempts to deflect some of the responsibility for the state of the school onto the district office and the Board of Education, he meets with disapproval from Stratton. Caught between contradictory demands of the parents, teachers, and his superiors, Dobson is in an impossible dilemma.

When he tries to moderate between conflicting parties or subtly change his line to favor those to whom he is talking, he is thought to be a two-timer and a phony. When he approaches all groups with the higher administrative rhetoric, he is considered an impersonal machine. Thus, whatever action Dobson takes, he further discredits himself in the eyes of his constituents.

Dobson would prefer to withdraw from all parties in the school by whom he is discredited. But he cannot, for he is daily faced with the responsibility of making and communicating decisions that vitally affect everyone. When forced to communicate a decision unfavorable to a person or group, he says he is sorry about what he has to do, that he would rather not do it, but that he has been forced to by other parties. When he fires a teacher, he maintains that he is acting on orders from Stratton or pressure from parents. When he suspends a child, he tells the parent that this is the province of the guidance counselor and he could do nothing to stop it. When he tells a teacher that a child is *not* being suspended, he cites pressure from the parents and the district office. When he blocks an innovation in the school that parents are demanding, he cites a rule from central headquarters. In almost any instance Dobson can appear as if he has no power, but is only an extension of other pressure groups and outside agencies. Through him and upon him, all the contradictions of Midway are played out. As head of his school, he symbolizes and expresses the failure of administrative bureaucracy in education.

Midway's administrators are caught in a crossfire of parental anger, supervisory dissatisfaction, teacher disrespect, and child rebellion. All their activity is directed toward ducking the crossfire. But in doing so they unintentionally administrate and sustain those policies which undermine the interests of parents and children. It is ironic but not illogical, given society's relationship to its lower-class youth, that the very activities which enable administrators to survive in the school insure the children's failure.

The Task of Guidance

As PART of the orientation of new teachers, Mrs. Talbot, the guidance counselor, gives a picture of her "role":

I'm just delighted to see you all here. I want to describe to you what my role is in relation to you and to the children. I'm sort of all around the building. I work on many fronts—with children, teachers, the principal and assistant principal, parents, and outside community agencies, like Welfare, foster homes, child guidance clinics, et cetera. I am the link between the school and the community.

How does my work affect you and how can you relate to me? I can show you how you can refer a child with a problem to me. The guidance counselor is not only interested in children who are discipline problems. This is a stereotype which must be cleared up immediately. I'm also interested in children who are withdrawn, truant, or may have speech defects.

I think we will establish a definite method of referral. And why can't you simply refer someone to me when you have a problem? Well, the administration wants to be aware of the problems too. And then with appropriate screening the most important problems are taken by me.

Now I need an anecdotal record form so I can have an adequate picture of how the child behaves. I want to see some kind of pattern emerging so if you tell me that a child is a pest or a brat, well this is sort of subjective don't you think? But if you have an anecdotal record which gives specific instances of abnormal behavior, it is more objective, and I can have some idea of what to do and what, if any, referral should be made.

Mrs. Talbot sees herself as a professional, but in fact, Dobson uses her as a buffer between himself and threatening parents or children.

Parents can often be seen storming into Midway demanding satisfaction concerning the treatment of their children. Whenever possible, the irate parent is "referred" to Mrs. Talbot for a "conference" in which she attempts to "work with" the parent in the hope that she can be "dealt with." This strategy of guidance was applied even to Mrs. Jackson. Talbot was given the assignment of "working with" Jackson in the hope that if Talbot could "establish a friendly relationship with Mrs. Jackson," her attitudes toward Dobson and the teachers would be tempered.

The deflection of parental anger toward Talbot enables Dobson to maintain some distance from parents, but there is a deeper and more subtle effect. The change in language with which the parents are confronted constitutes a variation on the administrative tone. Dobson relates to parents in a technical language that is meaningful only to those who live within the educational world. Since Midway's parents are marginal to this world, his language is meaningless to them. The parents want to know why their child has been suspended, why he was removed from class, why he is "being put in a dumber class," why he isn't reading, and why the teacher is "beating on him." The parents are unable to comprehend explanations that spring from considerations of stability in the school.

Mrs. Talbot's psychiatric language of guidance is a more

sophisticated way of handling this indignation. In dealing with them, Talbot uses two basic approaches. One is to allow the angry parent to let off steam. She listens sympathetically and provides "support." Implicit in this tactic is the notion that if the parent is allowed to express her "hostility" in a "context of acceptance," she will begin to "identify" with the guidance counselor and therefore have less inclination to attack the school.

The other approach is an interpretive one. The parents' criticisms of the school are redefined as their own personal problems. For example, if a parent feels that teachers are incompetent or are not concerned with the children, she is told that she is "projecting her own inadequacies about being a parent onto the school." Mr. Rosenberg, the part-time psychologist assigned to Midway, has extended the notion of parental projection into a general theory of the community. He maintains that when the community gets angry at the school, it is engaging in "community projection."

To take another example, if a parent maintains that her child is "talking back to the teacher" or "causing trouble in his class" because, in the parent's view, the child "doesn't respect the teacher," the guidance counselor maintains that the child is "unable to function in the classroom" because of "emotional problems" he is having stemming from the "home" and the "community." Thus, all parents' views which could threaten the school and make it accountable to the community for its actions are reversed into criticisms of the community. Critical perspectives on the organization and operation of the school are reduced to personal problems of parents.

With children the task of guidance is essentially the same. The goal is to achieve control through guidance procedures when the traditional classroom and administrative procedures do not work. Children who are labeled "disruptive" are referred to Mrs. Talbot. She either sees the child individually or places him in a "guidance group" run by a teacher on the guidance committee. Referral to guidance is made on the theory that if the child is free to express hostility toward the guidance teacher and the school, and perceives the guidance teacher as "accepting him," the child will "identify" with the guidance teacher and want to behave acceptably in the classroom.

When this and all other attempts at pacification of "disruptive" children fail, the guidance counselor herself is called in to legitimate a suspension. Getting a child suspended from Midway is a complex task and one must comply with all sorts of legalistic requirements. Mrs. Talbot has spent as many as thirty hours working up a brief for suspension. But aside from the paper work, suspensions in Midway School are sensitive political issues. Teachers favor and press for suspensions because they can get rid of uncontrollable children, but of course, parents are opposed because they see the school avoiding responsibility. Administration must mediate between the two groups. Dobson would like to suspend more children and improve his relations with the teachers. But since Stratton takes the part of the parents, his impulse to suspend children is inhibited. Too many suspensions serve as evidence that Dobson is not controlling his school. So, to the annoyance of teachers, Dobson goes to great lengths to avoid suspensions. However, when he does decide to suspend a child, not only the filling out of forms but also the placating of parents is assigned to Mrs. Talbot.

The task of guidance is to legitimate whatever is done to children and explain it to parents in ways that do not serve as an indictment of the school. The psychiatric liturgy of guidance consecrates Midway's policies.

The Task of Ameliorative Programs

Midway places great emphasis on special techniques, especially qualified personnel, and technological innovations for the solution of its problems. Aside from the guidance counselor and the part-time psychologist, Midway employs two teachers for "slow learners," a reading specialist, a librarian, a part-time speech therapist, a reading coordinator for the lower grades, and a "training coordinator" for the new teachers. Generally, new specialties are created to deal with emergencies. For example, the reading levels in Midway School had deteriorated to such a degree that an experienced teacher, Mrs. Rothblatt, was made lower-grade reading coordinator for the express purpose of administering the New Horizons reading program. New Horizons spelled out in huge detail a way of teaching reading in which every teacher would be doing the same thing at the same time. The program, which was initiated in the second grade, took about two or three hours out of every school day.

Again, control deteriorated to an almost unbearable degree. Stratton hired a retired principal, Mrs. Winters, and with great fanfare, announced to teachers that the inexperienced teachers would finally get the "training and support that they need." And when the new teacher-run guidance groups were begun, Dobson, with obvious pride and relief, announced to a P.T.A. meeting that the school had "found a way of giving disruptive children the special attention that they need" and that very shortly five guidance groups were to start.

The continual introduction of special services and innovative programs serves to maintain the notion that something is being done and that the school is changing and experimenting with its educational policy. During a period of six months, three major new programs were added and five specialists hired. The school becomes so involved in incorporating new programs and experts, learning the new techniques and vocabularies, advertising them over the media, and selling them to parents, that hardly anyone notices that nothing has changed. By continually switching into new programs before the previous innovations have run their course, the larger picture of stagnation and failure need not be faced.

Mr. Dobson is prototypical of this psychology. Dobson admits the existence of an emergency, but to his admission he adds that next week some alteration in the school will be finished or some new program is to be initiated which will ease the pressure. The new wing will be finished, enabling everybody to go on regular session; the school yard alteration is to be completed, allowing the children to play outside; the new guidance program will be initiated, absorbing disruptive children; more aides are to be hired and volunteer parents recruited to help patrol the halls and the lunchroom. So the teachers and parents are asked to "hold out a little longer." But often as not, far from relieving the desperate situation, the innovation creates new emergencies.

For example, after a delay of many months, the new wing was finally completed. There was a general feeling, encouraged by Dobson, that once everyone went on regular session from 9 A.M. to 3 P.M. instead of 8 to 12 and 12 to 4, many of the problems created by the overcrowded conditions and by the children having to be in the classroom for four unbroken hours would be alleviated. There would now be a lunch break, each teacher would have her own classroom, floater teachers would be responsible for teaching particular classes and subjects, there would be a full six-hour day for the children, and teachers would have time to teach the whole curriculum. With the occupation of the new wing, things were supposed to "settle down."

But the occupation intensified the emergency. Thirteen hundred children were in Midway, entering, leaving, and eating lunch in two shifts, now with twice as much space in which to operate. This addition meant that all the new hallways had to be patrolled and secured. Children roamed the halls freely, sometimes in large running packs. There were now twice as many exits, and it became much easier for Midway's children as well as the saboteurs from Porter Junior High School to enter and leave the building. Unsecured halls increased the harassment of classrooms by free-roaming children. With the same number of teachers, school aides, and parent volunteers, the situation became impossible.

The new lunchroom now had to handle 650 children at a time, with only one teacher and a few aides to supervise the lunch hours. The result was total chaos with children running around the tables, in and out of the lunchroom, fighting, and throwing food at each other. The P.T.A. attacked the new lunchroom with greater intensity than they had previously complained of the lack of space.

Those teachers who had obviously depended on assistant principals for help in classroom emergencies found that because of the physical distance of the new wing from the administrative offices, they could not get help as quickly or easily. So uncontrollable classes could create more than the usual disturbance. Sometimes a teacher with a class out of control found that all other teachers on her floor were out to lunch. The emergencies created by opening the new wing were more destructive to the stability of the school than the previous emergency.

But there is always a pronouncement that help is on its way in the immediate future, and teachers "hold out" again until the situation is partially rectified. In the case of the problems created by the new wing, more aides were to be hired and volunteers recruited to patrol the halls and lunchroom. That didn't work, but then the school year was almost over. Teachers would have two months to recharge, there would be some new staff in the fall, and new programs would be initiated. Chronic crises that are marginally bearable can be permanently withstood as long as the images of innovation and alleviation can be held in mind. Everyone vaguely senses that Midway's problems are unsolvable. But in order for the teachers to continue, short-range solutions must be thought up and believed in, and a desperate bravado holds the school together.

Public Relations

The administration attempts to improve Midway's image by holding class teas, open houses, conferences, and other events for the community in which the best work of the children is displayed, demonstration lessons are given by the most qualified and experienced teachers, and innovative programs are explained to parents. Whenever possible, the school attempts to get the mass media to cover these events. As one administrator put it, "There is nothing like a good press for improving the school." Administrators equate good public relations and the absence of external pressure with a good school.

Throughout the year the local press and television describe Midway's programs and offer the school as a model for other ghetto schools to emulate. One news story which was titled, "They're Learning to Read in Midway School," described the high qualifications of an "integrated staff" who "cooperated" in the education of the children. It closed with the point, "They're doing it here. Why can't all schools be like Midway?" If these innovative programs that portray Midway positively reach the parents, the community, or the public at large through the media, the school can try to counteract its negative image.

It is hard to sustain a positive image of Midway through the press. For every public relations coup that the administration makes, there is an article which points out the children's poor performance on standardized tests and the general lack of control. One article in a local paper described how the school had been broken into fifteen times during the year, the classrooms literally wrecked, and 150 windows broken. The opportunities for negative publicity outnumber by far the opportunities for a "good press."

When the teachers instituted a wildcat strike over the attempted firing of Rosen, the district office and the school administration were able to prevent the story from being leaked to the press. Likewise, when the P.T.A. and the local CORE and Black Muslims called a boycott and picketed outside the school, the event somehow did not reach the press. Since there are so many negative opportunities, administrators must work very hard to prevent the media from getting embarrassing information. Often, surprisingly, they succeed.

A good outcome to a community event is often dependent on the cooperation of the children. If the school's image is to be positive in the eyes of parents, educational officials, and other interested individuals, the children have to go along with the program and temporarily suspend their inclination to make the teachers and administrators look bad. So, for example, in the planning of demonstration lessons for parents, much time is spent in picking a teacher who is least likely to lose control of his class and a class that is most likely to accept control. Before important community events, Dobson makes spot announcements over the PA system asking the children to be on their best behavior as "Midway School will be on view."

Major public relations events are scheduled when the school is doing most poorly. Before one crucial open house, to which parents and several hundred administrators and officials were invited, Dobson spoke over the PA system for fifteen minutes begging the children not to sabotage the show. When the children caused no major disruptions, he thanked them over the PA system with greater emotion than anyone had seen him display for a long time.

The most important public relations event during the school year is the final open house in which the children's best work is displayed. The administration hypothesizes that if parents can be shown that the children are producing high quality work, it is proof that they are learning something. The problem for the staff is to present enough work covering all the curriculum areas to show that high quality work has been produced all year. About a month before the open house, teachers and administrators hold a meeting at which they discuss what kind of work in which grade and in which curriculum areas will be needed. The responsibility for gathering the work, most of which has not yet been produced, is divided up among the teachers, and they then go to the children to get it. The month before the open house is devoted almost totally to the mass production of "high quality work."

Guidance, ameliorative programs, and public relations all work to cool criticism of the school and justify administrative policy. In spite of psychiatric rhetoric, the new wing, New Horizons, or an occasional "good press," Midway's reputation progressively deteriorates. Teachers view boycotts, school riots, and angry confrontations with community militants on TV. They wonder when their own school will be the focus of the evening news.

CHAPTER XII

THE RACIAL DIMENSION
OF TEACHING

The Black Teacher's Administrative Task

MIDWAY'S nine Black teachers have a special problem. They have a large stake in the children's education. Most of the Black teachers approach their task with a fervor that few white teachers can sustain. They want to do something for their race, and they sympathize with the plight of the Black children. As one Black teacher stated it, "They're our children." But, as teachers, they are expected to protect the school and its staff from the children. The Black teacher has a conflict between his racial and occupational identity. The resolution of this conflict has far-reaching consequences for the stability of the school.

Like their white colleagues, Black teachers are concerned with doing a job. But in doing their job they have a natural advantage. Whatever children, parents, administrators, or teachers may feel about the way a Black teacher treats children, it is difficult to label him a racist. Thus a Black teacher is less inhibited in his discipline of children than his white colleagues.

> Well, I am very firm. I don't even allow watering. Even the kids who are good I give a rough time. I don't let

them get away with anything. If they don't do their homework, or if they forget to bring their books, I do something—I won't tell you what.

But later he was more candid.

Yes, I hit the kids. I do it on their hands, with a ruler. I do not do it maliciously, and I do it in front of the whole class. Occasionally a parent will come and say, "Did you hit my kid?" and I say, "Yes, I hit your kid," and they don't bother me. If I were to hem and haw, they would feel different. But I come right out with it and that psychs them out immediately. Now when I started—from the very start—I had no problems, either with the parents or the children, because I decided that I wasn't going to take any nonsense and I haven't. Eventually the parents realized that I was serious about working with the children, and they don't bother me. In fact they give me permission to do it. After a while, I didn't care who I hit.

This Black teacher attributes his disciplinary freedom to his dedication to working for the children rather than to his color.

In its calculus of survival Midway exploits the natural advantages of its Black teachers in answering the Black parents. For example, when Dobson became the target of Mrs. Jackson's tirade at P.T.A. meetings and Dobson was too flustered to answer, Mr. Johnson, the senior Black teacher, answered for him and defended the school:

I have been teaching in Midway for nine years. Now let me say that is is impossible to teach every subject every day. I teach language arts and math every day and social studies and science twice a week. I do the best I can as a teacher. Those of you who know me are aware that I am very strict with the children. But I get good results. It's a good feeling when the children who I had in 1960 come back and tell me how much I helped them. Now it is our job as teachers to do a job and teachers should be taken to task if they don't do their job. I have been trying my best for nine years and I hope I have the wisdom and the fortitude to continue, and the day I can no longer do a job I will stop coming. Now the fact that I am an experienced teacher doesn't necessarily mean that I am a good teacher. Some of the new teachers are more dedicated than the older teachers because they have to prove themselves and the older teachers, some of them, tend to rest on their laurels. The new teachers should be given a chance to show what they can do, and attacking them before they've had a chance doesn't do any good.

Johnson also defends Dobson when he is under personal attack. The previous year Mrs. Jackson had become so dissatisfied with Dobson that she called a school boycott. A meeting was immediately set up by Stratton in which the complaints of the community against Dobson could be aired. At the meeting attended by several hundred parents and all of the teachers, Johnson vigorously defended Dobson against Jackson's charges. As a result of Johnson's defense Dobson kept his job. As Johnson summed it up, "Something had to be said and if it wasn't said the right way, there could have been trouble."

Midway's teachers enlist the aid of Black teachers in their conflicts with the administration and the district office. Because of the Black teachers' indispensability to the school, the administrators are more likely to listen to them. On Stratton's orders, Dobson called a meeting to inform the teachers of the parents' grievances and of Stratton's threat that anyone would be fired who didn't do his job. Peters, the only Black acute teacher at Midway, defended his colleagues. Answering Dobson, he asserted that the administrators should "back up their staff instead of attacking them." As a result of his confrontation with Dobson, Peters gained the respect and admiration of the entire teaching staff. He became a teacher leader.

When Stratton and the parents attempted to fire Rosen a few weeks later, it was Peters who organized and led the

wildcat strike in which fifty of the seventy teachers participated. After Rosen was transferred, there was a series of
meetings with Stratton and the administration in which Peters
aggressively defended the teachers' interests. He soon began
to speak out vigorously in P.T.A. meetings whenever Mrs.
Jackson attacked the teachers, and he is thought to be responsible for getting her temporarily to tone down her attacks.
Peters rapidly became a crucial figure in every issue involving
teachers.

Peters, Johnson, and other Black teachers are thought to
be the only ones who can effectively defend the interests of
teachers and administrators against the parents and the district
office. They are known to be the most effective disciplinarians
with children. They may have criticisms of the school and may
be dissatisfied, but in situations where the vulnerable white
teachers and administrators are unable to defend themselves,
the Black teachers conduct the defense. Amidst ineffectiveness
and incompetence, they serve as an undercover leadership.
Unwittingly, their aggressiveness and articulateness are crucial
in maintaining the status quo in Midway.

Midway's Black teachers also run most of those assembly
meetings, fire drills, and other public ceremonies in which
patriotism, respect for constituted authority, affirmation of the
American way of life, and the celebration of democracy are
the themes. They usually lead the patriotic singing, organize
and direct the color guard, prepare and supervise the graduation exercise, and oversee the election of class representatives
and school officers. Implied in all of these public meetings,
coordinated marches, mass sings, and democratic elections is
the notion that Midway's children are Americans like everyone
else, derive all the benefits of citizenship, and hence should
respect the symbols of authority in the persons of teachers and
administrators. By running Midway's public ceremonies, the
Black teachers are instrumental in convincing the children that
they should be controlled.

The Ambiguity of Being Black

Midway's Black teachers are aware of their indispensability to white teachers and administrators. But they are in turn dependent on the acceptance and appreciation of their white colleagues. This dependence is related in part to an image of middle-class life which they attribute to white teachers and attempt to emulate. The Black teachers are characteristically neat, clean, self-disciplined, and economical in speech and movement. They talk with their white colleagues about sports cars, stocks, the rebellious children, and the uncouth parents. Some caricature a middle-class life style. They sincerely believe in middle-class values—a belief that is not shared by many white teachers who are cynical about commitment and the American way of life and everything they are required to do in the school.

Some Black teachers view their white colleagues as comrades-in-arms. Having seen battle together with the children, many feel as if they are members of the same platoon. It becomes crucial for Black teachers to avoid anything that would interfere with this image of their relationship with white teachers. Black teachers rarely criticize white teachers or cross them in public. A Black teacher criticized a white teacher to a third party and the white teacher found out and asked the Black teacher about it. The Black teacher went to great extremes attempting to convince his white colleague that he "meant no criticism." The unwillingness of Black teachers to criticize white teachers stems from more than their desire to be accepted by them. Midway's Black teachers operate under a psychology of occupational scarcity. Many entered teaching when civil service jobs were the only ones they could get with a college degree. For them, teaching has been a way into the middle class. The Black teacher is always in a defensive position because his desire for professional acceptance always exceeds his desire to identify with Blacks.

White teachers are ambivalent toward their Black colleagues. Like the administrators, they are impressed with the
Black teacher's commitment and are grateful for the disproportionate amount of work they do. Any white teacher or
administrator will freely admit that the Black teachers "more
than do a job." At the same time there is much resentment
of the Black teachers' disciplinary advantage. As one white
teacher said, "You know they can say things to the kids that
you can't—like 'I'll beat your butt.'" Another put it, "When
I hit a child, I'm a racist. When a Black teacher hits a child,
he's doing it for his own good."

But the Black teachers make the less effective white teachers'
jobs so much easier that, from the white teachers' perspective,
it does not pay to harbor too much ambivalence. Some of the
white teachers identify totally with the "strength" of the Black
teachers. Like many of the children they exaggerate the un-
challengeable authority of certain Black teachers. ("He looks
rough. He isn't big, but he looks rough.") This adulation is
closely related to the white teachers' identification with Black
athletes. Often their conversations shift back and forth between the exploits of famous Black athletes and the feats of
Black teachers in Midway. One white teacher even harbors
sadistic fantasies about what he and a well-known Black
teacher will do to a recalcitrant child. "One day me and Smith
will get Sammy in one of the supply rooms and we'll beat
the shit out of him, but we'll do it so there won't be any
marks."

In the heat of their experience in Midway, many white
teachers express feelings about children in the presence of
Black teachers. In doing so they do not forget that the teachers
are Black. But the white teachers view Black teachers only as
colleagues and find it difficult to entertain the idea that Black
teachers might in some instances identify with the children.
One Black teacher flinched ever so slightly when he heard a
white colleague describe his own class as a "zoo." He quickly

recovered and acted as if nothing had happened. The Black teachers are treated as if they didn't have a conflict of interest and respond to white teachers as if there were none.

The Black teachers have a conflict between their desire to identify with the children and their desire to be accepted as competent professionals by their white colleagues and superiors. Many Black teachers resolve this problem by suppressing their Black consciousness beneath their adult- or teacher-consciousness. They do the job that ingratiates them with their white colleagues and pursue a style which is a caricature of middle class sobriety. But in attempting to resolve the conflicting demands of profession and race, they execute many of Midway's policies which Midway's white administrators by themselves could never sustain.

The Risk of Being White

The white teacher is aware of racial pressure in everything he does at Midway. He is always worried about being viewed as a racist by children, parents, and colleagues. Many are concerned with their self-evaluation. All white teachers, even those who have no doubts about their lack of racism, must be careful in their relations with children. A white teacher who is about to strike a child either closes the classroom door and pulls the window shade or does it in a part of the classroom that cannot be seen easily by a passer-by. White teachers consciously treat with kid gloves all those children whose parents are active in the P.T.A. or are known to be especially sensitive to how their children are treated by white teachers.

In their activity with black children, the white teachers take a good deal of risk. For many, practically anything they do which is crucial to the maintenance of control can be grounds for being called a racist or being fired. Much of what is generally considered to be "part of the job" is formally illegal if not subjectively immoral. Hence, many white teachers view their job in Midway as underground activity. The white teacher has to shift his behavior depending on his audience. To parents and administrators he has to appear as if his relations with the children were legal. He can stage his brutality only when administrators, parents, and certain teachers are not present.

Even those white teachers who are no longer concerned with the moral implications of their activity feel that they are in a dangerous situation. One white teacher was transferred for whipping a child with a rope. He was indignant over his transfer and contended that he alone had been singled out for punishment when "everybody hits the children." When such an exposure occurs, the white teacher often feels that he is being discriminated against.

For many white teachers, doing a job involves a total betrayal of their sense of morality. The problem for the self-conscious white teacher is to perform successfully those tasks necessary to survival without so violating his ethics that he cannot live with himself. This difficulty is often resolved by an attitude which white liberal teachers as well as Black teachers cultivate toward the children. In Midway, children are almost universally viewed by adults as second-class citizens with few natural rights, and this view is not considered racist.

From the perspective of Midway's adults, there are two kinds of children: "good children" and "bad children." A good child is one who is obedient and a bad child is one who is not. Almost anything can be said or done to a child in the interest of making him a "good child." Thus it is legitimate for liberal white teachers to take a morally indignant attitude toward the "disruption" of bad children. But this simplification of the teacher-child relationship is complicated by the whiteness of the teachers and the blackness of the children. It becomes difficult for liberal white teachers to take an unambiguously self-righteous stance toward Black children.

Many white teachers resolve their racial dilemmas by denying the children's Blackness and insisting that they are only children, and, in so doing can interpret their color blindness as proof of their lack of racism. When speaking to administrators, parents, and other teachers, they consciously use phrases like "the children," "that child," "those children," "your child." Those white teachers who regularly denigrate and brutalize the children would like to forget that they were doing it to Black children.

Black teachers and parents who would like to feel that the white teachers are not racist also attempt to convince each other that "children are children." In conversations between white teachers, Black teachers, and parents, the childishness of the children is compulsively exaggerated. Implied is an almost desperate attempt on the part of Midway's adults to define and redefine the basis on which punishment of the children can be justified. All of the efforts at avoiding the racial dimension of the children can be seen as an attempt by teachers, parents, and administrators to live with each other in a situation where violence toward Black children by white teachers is an everyday fact of life. The extremes to which Midway's adults will go to maintain their coalition against the children is indicative of their fear of lack of control.

BEHIND the rhetorical facade, in which everything is supposed to be done in the name of the children, lies a reality of teachers, administrators, and parents pursuing their political interests in Midway School. Within the self-justifying adherence to the values of education, teachers, parents, and administrators, in battles and coalitions with each other, attempt to come to terms with the realities of life in the school and turn them into explicit personal opportunities. These personal strivings and class struggles affect crucially the tone of the school and the lives of its participants.

The Image of the Past

Until five years ago Midway School was considered by its teachers and administrators to be a good school. Indeed, it had a reputation as one of the best schools in the district. Much of Midway's success from the standpoint of its staff was attributed to Kerner who was a strong principal, ran a tight school, and instilled discipline and loyalty in his teachers. But the past success is also thought to be related to the cooperation of parents and children.

Parental involvement during the Kerner administration was

limited to participation in the planning and execution of class teas, open houses, carnivals, and science fairs. Teachers from the Kerner administration can often be heard reminiscing about all the joint projects that they initiated with the parents and the freedom from surveillance by parents. According to the teachers, the parents were more cooperative because they were less significantly involved in Midway's affairs.

The Change in Administration

In 1963 Dobson became principal in the midst of a large-scale awakening of ghetto community militancy and heightened racial sensitivity. Dobson's personality aggravated these potential problems. Midway School quickly "loosened up." Teachers ran their classes as they pleased without fear of his interference. He spent most of his time in his office. Children began to take liberties with impunity that they would not have dared to take under Kerner. It quickly became common knowledge that control over the children pretty much began and ended with the personal competence of the teacher. As the effects of the decline of central authority spread, the children pressed their advantage. Irreverence, disruption, and breakdown in control spread from a few isolated classes to the hallways, the lunchroom, the gym, the assembly hall, and the schoolyard. Over the next few years Midway "deteriorated" in the minds of teachers, administrators, and parents from one of the best schools in the district to one of the worst.

The Radicalization of the P.T.A.

Mrs. Jackson, who was elected president of the P.T.A. in the fall of 1966, instituted policies of direct confrontation with administration and of harassment of teachers (whom she sometimes labeled as "foreigners"). Aside from patrolling the halls and spying on teachers in their classrooms, she would also check the teachers' punch-in cards daily to see which teachers were late and absent. She also developed relationships with the secretarial staff, the cleaning women, the janitorial staff, and the school aides, all of whom acted as her intelligence agents. Finally she encouraged the dissatisfied parents to tell her any complaints they had against teachers or administrators. With a small but aggressive clique of parents, Jackson in a very short time developed a far-reaching and fairly reliable intelligence network. She could present specific and detailed evidence to Dobson in his office, to the parents in P.T.A. meetings, and to Stratton in the district office when she failed to get satisfaction from Dobson.

Previous to Jackson's election, the P.T.A. had traditionally functioned as the public relations agency of the school administration. Via the P.T.A., the administration could show that parents were involved in the education of their children and were cooperating with the teachers. There was no traditional way for parents to voice their grievances. In effect, teachers and administrators were totally insulated from contact with the community on other than their own terms. Mrs. Jackson, through her aggressive personality, her dominance of the P.T.A., and her organizational ability focused parental anxiety and hostility on the school and its personnel. Where, before, the parents portrayed themselves as passive and apathetic, they were now dissatisfied and militant. Jackson symbolized this new militancy and, through her position in the P.T.A., revolutionized traditional politics in Midway School.

Teachers held Dobson responsible for protecting them from Jackson, and wanted him to "stand up to the parents." But Dobson was as terrified of Jackson as the teachers were. This inability to deal with Jackson was not just a personality problem. His immediate superior in the district office, Stratton, had become aware of the parents' new militancy. He sought out Mrs. Jackson and after a "long series of talks" concluded that he could "work with her" and that it was the responsibility of the administrators and teachers in Midway to work with her also. He wrote a position paper arguing that the principal and teachers should welcome the parents into the school, should listen to their complaints and suggestions, and, in general, should communicate and cooperate with the community. Also, he encouraged Jackson to come to his office whenever she could not get satisfaction from Dobson. By listening to and sympathizing with her complaints, Stratton avoided becoming an object of her attack. The responsibility for the present state of the school and for implementing the changes was passed to Dobson.

Dobson was then put in the position of having to seek an accommodation with Jackson. But an accommodation with Jackson on her terms would have meant the firing or transfer of many teachers and a degree of surveillance and supervision of the rest which they were prepared to go to great lengths to resist. For they had by this time become accommodated to a "loose school." Dobson was trapped, and so, whenever Jackson complained and asked for innovations, he responded by explaining to her in as bland and as rational a way as possible why he could not institute her requests because of rules set down by the Board of Education and the district office. Jackson would return to Stratton, who would sympathize with her, talk about how parents should be communicated with, and send her back to Midway. With each incident Stratton appeared more and more to Jackson to be a concerned ally while Dobson appeared to be an intransigent defender of the status quo.

The Spring Boycott

By the spring semester of 1967, Jackson had realized that while she and the parents had made their point and had shaken up the school, Dobson was not instituting any of their demands and that there was no way they could force him to do so. Jackson concluded that the only viable change left was Dobson's departure. She also realized that the campaign against the teachers and Dobson lacked focus. She needed an issue that would generate enough community opinion against Dobson to get him fired or transferred.

She eventually seized upon the issue of books. Parents claimed that many classes were without decent books. Actually, many of the teachers didn't use the books they had. Their reason for not using them was that the children were two years behind in reading and could not read the books issued at their present grade level.

Jackson demanded that since the teachers were not teaching the children anything anyhow, all children should at least have a new modern book in each subject so that they could take the books home and have their parents teach them. The book issue became the object of a well-organized campaign in which flyers were sent out to parents and local civil rights groups were contacted. Negotiations were set up by a committee between the parents, the administration, and the teachers to try to settle the book problem.

In the midst of the negotiations, a few days before the onset of summer vacation, Jackson called a school boycott. On June 23, when teachers and children came to school, they found a picket line consisting of Jackson and her P.T.A. clique, a group of children, representatives from the local CORE chapter, and Black Muslims dressed in African clothing. They carried signs which read "Dobson must Go," "Save our Children," "Black Teachers for Black Children," "We want Decent Books," and "White Teachers go Home." Approximately fifty per cent of the children refused to cross the picket line. Black teachers who crossed the line were castigated by some of the picketers for not wearing African clothing and for their collusion with the "white colonialists."

The district office and Midway's administration attempted to break the coalition of the P.T.A. and the Black militant civil rights groups. Stratton invited the leaders of CORE and the Black Muslims into the school. Apparently Jackson, who had been attending CORE meetings, had convinced the leadership that there was less education, and more brutality occurring in Midway than in the other schools in Randolph Park. But when the Black militant civil rights leaders walked into the school, they found half-empty classes under control. The leaders of CORE withdrew their people from the picket line the following day. Stratton maintained that they had even apologized. At the same time Dobson produced a group of parents who had dominated the P.T.A. before Jackson's election. They maintained that they were opposed to the boycott and the actions of the P.T.A. because these activities were interfering with the education of their children.

The exodus of CORE and the Black Muslims and the appearance of parents friendly toward the administration had no effect on Jackson. She continued to demand that Dobson be replaced and continued to man the picket line. At the suggestion of Stratton, a public meeting was held the following evening to hear the grievances of the P.T.A. and the charges against Dobson. The meeting, which was held in the school auditorium, was attended by about 300 parents and Midway's entire teaching and administrative staff. After Mrs. Jackson gave a longer tirade than usual, Mr. Johnson spoke in defense of Dobson and the teachers. As a result of the hearing a much bigger slice of the school budget was allocated for books.

By the fall of 1967 many classes had new books, and teachers were instructed to have the children bring them home every night. But since the new books were written for children with a reading level commensurate with their grade, bringing them home each day became nothing more than a public relations sop for the parents.

As a result of the parental pressure and the boycott, the administration told the teachers not to write letters home to parents. The letters written by teachers were replaced by form letters that covered every possible situation in the school. Form letters were devised and mimeographed for lateness, absenteeism, fighting in class, refusal to do homework, and general lack of cooperation. The rationale for the form letters was that parents had become "extremely sensitive" to what teachers said and thus might "misconstrue" something written by a teacher.

So, following the boycott, school policy became almost totally oriented to Mrs. Jackson. The administration spent most of its energy the following term trying to devise ways of coopting, neutralizing, or discrediting Jackson, as well as devising public relations projects to counter Jackson's image of the school. The guidance counselor was assigned to work with her. A concerted effort was made to bring more favorably disposed parents into the P.T.A. An unusually large number of class teas, open houses, and demonstrations of the New Horizons reading program was planned and executed to show that teachers and parents were "working together for the good of the children."

At the same time, events beyond everyone's control were happening, which heightened the already strained relations between the P.T.A. and the staff.

The Fall Strike

When the school resumed in the fall of 1967, the teachers' union called a city-wide strike that lasted for about three weeks. About fifty-five of the seventy teachers honored the picket line. Of the fifteen teachers who reported for work, eleven had never taught before. They crossed the picket line because they had taken teaching jobs to avoid the war in Vietnam and feared they would lose their occupational deferments if they struck. Thus, fifteen teachers, mostly inexperienced, were faced with the problem of controlling anywhere from 500 to 1100 children.

The general effect of the strike on the school was to give

the children a distinct advantage in asserting their options and to furnish the militant parents with further evidence of the incompetence of the staff. When the strike was over and the teachers returned to work, it immediately became evident that much of the disruptive behavior facilitated by the strike would be continued. Thirty of the teachers had never taught before. Encouraged by their experiences during the strike and cognizant of the inexperience of the new teachers, the children made historic gains in the ratio of uncontrolled to controlled classes. In the first month after the conclusion of the strike, approximately eleven of the thirty-two classes in the second through the sixth grades were seriously out of control. Many other classes were on the borderline.

The breakdown in control aided and abetted the P.T.A.'s attack on the teachers and administrators. The children's disruption provided unmistakable evidence that the teachers were incompetent and not doing their job, and the administration was unwilling or incapable of forcing them to do so. Jackson pressed her case against the teachers in the P.T.A. meetings. She charged that the classrooms were "disgraceful," that the teachers were not teaching the curriculum or using the new books. The administration countered that the teachers were inexperienced, that they "needed training," that they should be "given a chance," that it would be difficult to maintain control and teach the entire curriculum until the new wing would be finished and the school could go off triple session. Jackson replied that the money allotted for training the inexperienced teachers could be better spent hiring teachers from the Afro-American Teaching Association to set up reading clinics after school. Further, she claimed that it was not just a question of inexperience. Many of the new teachers were just sitting in the back of the room doing nothing and had bad attitudes toward the children. She concluded that the children could not wait until these teachers "got experience" or "tried harder."

Throughout the fall semester relations between teachers and children further deteriorated. As the children's rebellion and the attacks of Mrs. Jackson and the parents intensified, the desperate teachers resorted more and more to corporal punishment as a means of control. About a month before the Christmas vacation the conflict between parents and teachers came to a head when a teacher was accused of hitting a child.

The Rosen Incident

In late November, Rosen, a new white teacher, was accused by Mrs. Jackson of pushing a first-grade child against the wall. The regular teacher, Mrs. Kramer, had gone to the washroom, leaving the class uncovered. Rosen was on hall duty at the time, heard a lot of commotion coming from the classroom, went in to see what was happening, and discovered Donald running around the room. Rosen chased him. Donald ended up with five stitches in his head.

Rosen claimed that he had tried to restrain the child, had caught him, held onto him, but the child had slipped away from his grasp and knocked his head against the wall. The parents claimed that Rosen had pushed or thrown Donald against the wall. The testimony of the children differed depending on who was questioning them.

Immediately after the incident, Rosen was called into Dobson's office to give his side of the story and then was sent to Stratton's office. Stratton told Rosen that he would "back him up" but warned that if Mrs. Jackson got wind of the incident, there might be trouble.

The next morning Mrs. Jackson stormed into the school followed by Donald's parents, the other officers of the P.T.A., a few members of the local board, and Stratton. There was a tense conference among Dobson, Stratton, Jackson, and Donald's parents outside Dobson's office. Amidst much animated conversation, Stratton was heard to declare that teachers who hit children would not be tolerated. They all went into Dobson's office and Rosen was called in. Rumor quickly spread to the effect that Rosen was about to be fired for unprofessional conduct. Several teachers had heard Stratton exclaim with much emphasis, as he was walking down the hall with Jackson, that he would "fire any teacher who laid a hand on any child in his district." The previous day Mrs. Kramer had been fired for not covering her class. Later in the morning, Rosen emerged from Dobson's office and told several teachers, including Peters, that he had been suspended from his class and would formally be fired by the end of the day.

The Wildcat Strike

Stratton's decision to fire Rosen angered a large group of acute teachers, many of whom were Rosen's friends. These late-session teachers, who did not have responsibility for the children until 12 p.m., gathered in the teachers' lunchroom to plan a course of action. The consensus of the lunchroom meeting was that "if they could do this to Rosen, they could do it to anybody." Peters, who was more enraged than anyone, declared, "If we don't stand together now, we might as well give up." All concurred that if they did not "stand up for Rosen," no one would be safe from the parents.

After much heated discussion it was decided to take Peters' suggestion that they circulate a petition to the teachers. The petition stated that since Rosen was being fired without a hearing and a precedent was being set that affected the security of every teacher in the school, the teachers would not pick up their classes in the afternoon until Rosen was reinstated and given a hearing. While the petition was being drawn up and circulated, an *ad hoc* committee consisting of Peters, Miss Blake, the union representative, and three other teachers, confronted Stratton, Jackson, and the parents with the teachers' opposition. By 11:45 A.M. the committee had been told in no uncertain terms that Rosen's firing would not be postponed or reversed. Fifty-two of the seventy teachers had signed the petition. The teachers held a brief meeting and decided that they had enough support to go ahead with the work stoppage.

At 12 P.M. the thirty-five teachers who man the late-session classes went to meet the children in the assembly hall but they merely stood by their classes and refused to take them upstairs. In the meantime, the *ad hoc* committee notified Stratton that the work stoppage had begun, that it had the backing of the teachers' union and most of the teachers, and that it would continue until Rosen's dismissal was postponed and he was granted a hearing. At the news of the work stoppage, Stratton was visibly upset and muttered comments about the union. Even so, he held firm in his intention to fire Rosen; he declared that his mind was made up, that his decision was final, and he demanded that the teachers take the children up to their classes. For two hours the teachers remained in the assembly hall with the children, who grew restless and started making a lot of noise, running around in the assembly hall and out into the halls. The situation became so desperate that early-session teachers on their lunch hour had to be deployed to help secure the assembly hall and the surrounding areas which were now approaching riot conditions.

At 2 P.M. after frantic conversations with his administrative assistant, Mr. Golden, Stratton told the *ad hoc* committee that he was going to "reopen the Rosen case." Several members of the *ad hoc* committee and Mr. Morton rushed into the assembly hall, conveyed the news, and told the teachers to take their classes upstairs. By 3 P.M. it was learned that Stratton had agreed to hold a hearing the following day in which two teachers and two members of the local board would "weigh all the evidence" and reach a decision that would be final.

The next morning the committee of Mr. Peters and Mrs. Dagastino representing the teachers and Reverend Williams and Mrs. Rivers from the local board heard from five children in Donald's class. To the annoyance of Peters and Mrs. Dagastino, Stratton kept interrupting the hearing to confer privately with Reverend Williams and Mrs. Rivers. Late in the afternoon, with the hearing still in progress, he called Rosen into his office and offered to transfer him to a school in another district where he could "start over with a clean record." When a relieved Rosen accepted the offer, Stratton again interrupted the hearing to tell the committee that Rosen had accepted a transfer. Peters and Dagastino protested the decision and the violation of what they thought had been a procedural pact. Stratton replied that as district superintendent he had to do what he thought was best for the good of the school. He then added that Donald's father had threatened to beat up Rosen the previous day, and he had decided that for Rosen's safety he would have to go to another school. He then praised Rosen for having "acted as professionally as he could for an inexperienced teacher."

From the perspective of the teachers, Stratton's unauthorized compromise transfer of Rosen was a victory for the parents. The teachers felt that the parents would see the transfer as tantamount to dismissal. The teachers' response ranged from mild disappointment with Rosen, who had deflated the only clear-cut fighting issue they had, to bitter rage at Stratton who had tricked them when they thought they had the upper hand.

The Attack on Stratton

By forcing a compromise that was acceptable to the parents and accepted under duress by teachers, Stratton had gotten himself off the hook without significant damage to his position in the school. For he had maintained his control over the local board and the confidence of Mrs. Jackson and the other militant parents. But in doing so he had totally alienated the teachers, who were still angry and wanted satisfaction.

The plan of Peters and the new militant teachers was to "confront" Stratton and "show him" that they "weren't going to be pushed around anymore." Stratton consented to meet with the teachers. They held several meetings without him and drew up a list of grievances to be mimeographed and distributed and to serve as an agenda for the confrontation. Mr. Peters, Mrs. Dagostino, Mrs. Bloomfield, and Mr. Martin were elected to be a panel of teachers in the otherwise open meeting.

There was some opposition to this approach to Stratton from Johnson who, when asked, refused to serve on the committee. Throughout this crisis, Johnson maintained a pessimistic attitude toward the confrontation declaring that he had tried to "move Stratton in the past" and that the teachers wouldn't get anywhere, and that it would "just be held against those who participated in the future."

In the meeting the following Friday, Stratton used his position of authority and all his administrative skills to prevent the confrontation. Upon arriving, he immediately set a time limit of an hour and a half, demanded that Dobson attend, chaired the meeting and talked ninety per cent of the time. Any issues that were raised were defined by Stratton as either illegitimate, Dobson's responsibility, or beyond his power to do anything about.

To the charge that Stratton was aiding and abetting the harassment by Jackson, he replied that it was his responsibility to talk to her when Dobson couldn't help her. To the charge that he was responsible for the low morale of teachers, he replied that Dobson was the head of the school and responsible for teacher-administration, and teacher-parent relations. To the charge that he had betrayed the teachers by transferring Rosen when he had agreed to a hearing, he replied that he did it for the good of the school and Rosen's physical safety. At the same time he appealed to the guilt of the teachers, after each series of complaints, by asking them how many really thought they were doing the best job they could. Finally, when asked for more specialized personnel, he replied that he had gotten a retired principal to be "teacher training coordinator." When the response was less than enthusiastic, Stratton threatened to have her withdrawn if the teachers didn't appreciate it. By monopolizing and controlling the meeting through administrative manipulation, shifting responsibility, refusing to discuss potentially damaging points, and general bluster and intimidation, Stratton turned a potentially debilitating confrontation into an administrative victory.

The Accommodation with Jackson

Defeated by Stratton, the disheartened teachers concentrated on the P.T.A. Peters, Martin, and other leaders of the wildcat strike started attending P.T.A. meetings regularly and "standing up" to Jackson when she attacked the teachers and school. Peters even went so far as to mispronounce her name ("Mrs. Jack") when she mispronounced his ("Mr. Pete"). After a series of exchanges Jackson began to trust Peters and began to take her complaints directly to him as she had previously done to Stratton. Peters persuaded Jackson that nothing would be accomplished while she attacked the inexperienced teachers, that "parents and teachers should cooperate with each other for the good of the school," and that Midway's real problem was the control of "rebellious children who make it impossible to teach" and the apathy of their "parents who just let their children run wild and bring down the school."

Persuaded by Peters, Jackson initiated a moratorium on attacking teachers and organized a joint committee of parents and teachers on the problem of "disruptive children." In subsequent P.T.A. meetings, Jackson shifted her attack to the behavior of the children and their irresponsible parents. Her diatribes remained long and emotional but they carefully avoided any strong criticism of the teachers who were even occasionally sympathized with for "the difficult job" they were trying to do. Groups of parents were recruited to walk the halls and enter classrooms for the purpose of bawling out uncontrolled classes and getting the names of student leaders. In a few weeks Peters had done what the administrators had not been able to do in a year and a half.

The New Wing and Intensified Sabotage

In March the new wing containing a lunchroom and about twenty new classrooms was completed, and Midway went back on single session. Parents assumed that the new wing and the full day would "settle the children down" and enable the teachers to "teach the full curriculum." The school had waited for the completion of the wing just as a besieged garrison waits for supplies and reinforcements.

Upon completion of the wing, the problems of securing the school intensified, for there was now twice as much area to secure and the same number of teachers. The new lunchroom now had to accommodate 1300 children in two periods with disastrous results. Children ran unhindered through the lunchroom screaming, fighting, and throwing food. Jackson announced that the teachers in the lunchroom had "tried" but it was "out of their hands." She called for more parent volunteers and got them, but they failed to alter the riot conditions, which rapidly spilled over into the halls. After eating, the children ran through the school, often in gangs, stopping only to fight, harass occupied classrooms, and eat their gum and candy; and for the most part, they were ignored by teachers passing by on their way to lunch.

As children's security in the halls increased, property sabotage grew worse. With increasing regularity false fire alarms were sounded, classroom windows were broken, bathroom floors were urinated and defecated upon, and bulletin-boards were desecrated. The new wing had doubled the number of bulletin-boards. Democratic slogans and pictures of children from different races cooperating together were torn down immediately and replaced by pornographic slogans and imagery. Several bulletin-boards were set on fire.

The contractors who built the new wing had not yet put the protective screening over the windows. Within a week, 150 of the 200 new glass windows had been shattered. Soon after that, the school began to be broken into on weekends. Door windows were broken, desks and chairs overturned, books and other school supplies were ripped up and scattered over the rooms. Paint and ink were splashed on the walls and ceilings. Teachers and administrators would return each Monday to find the school in a shambles. With each weekend the sabotage intensified until on the final weekend before the end of the spring term, every classroom was broken into as well as the library, where most of the books were thrown in the middle of the floor, covered with ink, and many of them stuck to the floor with glue.

The Organization of the Children

Toward the end of the spring term a youth group called "We March Together" rented a basement of a brownstone across the street from the school and started recruiting children from Midway and Porter Junior High. Run by a Black drop-out from Columbia University, "We March Together" was organized on a quasi-military basis. Loyalty to leaders, called lieutenants and captains, was stressed as well as "Black pride." Many of the meetings were spent in learning fancy drill, which was displayed whenever possible in Midway's classrooms. Within a few weeks, "We March Together" had recruited about 100 children from Midway and about 300 from Porter Junior High. Before the end of the term, "We March Together" was in serious competition with the local "PAL" group (a youth group sponsored by the police department) and the WMT drill team had performed in a school assembly. The plan of WMT, according to its leaders, was to organize and discipline as many of Midway's children as possible, and at the proper time to take some sort of collective action such as a school boycott. Sensing this, teachers and administrators tried to discourage interested children from joining WMT and offered PAL as an alternative.

The P.T.A. Election

Mrs. Bordon, a Black "parent involvement coordinator" for District 7 working out of Stratton's office, had regularly attended Midway's P.T.A. meetings. A month before the end of the spring term, she suggested at a meeting that since there had not been an election held for two years and Mrs. Jackson had "borne the burden of parent involvement practically alone," there should be an election. Mrs. Rothblatt, a chronic teacher active with parents, picked a slate of parents to run for office. The ones she selected had been active in the P.T.A. before Mrs. Jackson's administration and were known for their past cooperation with Midway's administrative and teaching staff. Mrs. Bordon then took on the task of persuading Mrs. Jackson to retire as president so that "the burden could be shared." The election was scheduled for the next P.T.A. meeting. But when Mrs. Jackson told Mrs. Bordon the day before the meeting that she would leave the decision of her retirement up to the parents, and when a few teachers offered to show up for the meeting, fearing that Jackson might be nominated and even win, Dobson cancelled the meeting on the grounds that neither he, Morton, nor Ryley could make it.

The election was held two weeks later. About fifty parents, Mrs. Bordon, Mr. Morton, Miss Ryley, and fifteen teachers attended. After the speeches of the nominees, Mrs. Bordon, who was chairing the meeting, quickly said, "If there are no other nominations we will move to vote for president." A parent got up and nominated Mrs. Jackson. Bordon reminded the parents that Jackson had served two years and needed some help and then immediately called for a vote without allowing Jackson to speak. The vote was Mrs. Andrews 42, Jackson 28. All of the teachers and administrators but one voted for Mrs. Andrews. After the election for president, Jackson was nominated for and elected vice-president. In her scheduled farewell address, Jackson declared "I don't care if I'm vice-. I'll keep on fighting for the children."

The Exit of Dobson, Morton, and Ryley

During the summer of 1968, Dobson informed Stratton that he was applying for an early sabbatical and under no conditions would he ever return to Midway School. Stratton attempted to talk Morton into becoming interim principal, but he had already obtained a transfer as assistant principal in a junior high school outside of Randolph Park, as had Miss Ryley to an elementary school. Stratton, using his emergency powers, appointed Mr. Johnson (the senior Black teacher) to be assistant principal and one of his own coordinators, Mrs. Williams (also Black), to be principal. Parents, teachers, and children assumed Dobson had been fired in spite of Stratton's explanations. Before introducing Mrs. Williams to the teachers the next fall, Stratton exhorted, "We all have a wonderful new opportunity to work for the children. Now I know you all have feelings about the past, but we could argue about that for a long time and not get anywhere. So let's get on with the job and leave Midway's past to the historians."

The character of internal politics at Midway can be seen as a response to two major events in Midway's recent history: (1) The breakdown in centralized administrative leadership in Dobson's administration. (2) The rising community militancy as symbolized in the person of Mrs. Jackson and by the irreverent and rebellious children. In their various attempts to maximize their opportunities, all of Midway's major participants, administrators, teachers, parents, children must respond in one way or another to these two major events.

As district superintendent, Stratton has to appear to be controlling his district and meeting the needs of the community. Midway's weak local administration, militant parents, and rebellious children complicated these goals. Anticipating the time when he may be more directly accountable to community pressure, Stratton attempted to create a constituency for himself among frustrated militant parents by catering to their frustrations and by ingratiating himself with Mrs. Jackson. By appearing to be sympathetic to parental concerns and reminding them that Dobson was responsible for Midway, Stratton was able to avoid a major clash with parents. But in taking the side of the parents during the Rosen incident he could not avoid a major clash with the teachers.

Whatever their quarrel with the Board of Education bureaucracy, teachers would rather be accountable to it than to the parents. For the educational system asks nothing more of Midway's teachers than the control of the children. In a situation where the children are not being educated and illegal measures are being used to control them, the educational bureaucracy and the union were the only source of protection from the demands of the militant parents. But Midway's teachers' union was politically inactive and held meetings only in the midst of school crises. For the most part, chronic union teachers were resigned to the weakness of Dobson, the militancy of Jackson, and the double-dealing of Stratton. They discouraged the acute teachers from acting aggressively toward Stratton or Jackson. The policy of Midway's teachers is to exploit the immunity from accountability that the educational bureaucracy provides them and to organize only when that immunity is seriously threatened. But this essentially passive stance puts them in a defensive and disadvantaged position when crises occur.

The Rosen incident was such a threat to their immunity. But even during crises of this magnitude, the chronic teachers fear Stratton and refuse to organize opposition or to represent teachers' interests. During the Rosen incident and the clash with Stratton, Peters and the other acute teachers had to act without benefit of the chronic teachers' experience and could not sustain any political organization. Although Stratton had made a serious mistake in miscalculating the teachers' response, he was able to outmaneuver and intimidate his inexperienced opponents and got through the crisis without significant damage to his position in the school or to his hold on the district. Discouraged by their intimidating confrontation with Stratton, Peters and a few other teachers then concentrated on containing Jackson.

Midway's parents under the leadership of Jackson are able to carry out a sustained attack on the school. But Midway's parents operate from a conception of education which bears no relationship to Midway's educational reality. Like Midway's teachers and administrators, they are convinced that if somehow the school is controlled, the teachers teach, and assignments are made in books, the children will learn, go to high school and college, and get decent jobs. In their attitude toward education they are seduced by the very teachers and administrators whom they want to replace. Parental attitudes toward education also have the effect of diluting their attack on the school. Midway's parents can only be effective politically if the school is in a state of chaos. The more uncontrolled the classes are, the more the parents can point to the ineffectiveness and incompetence of Midway's staff. Therefore, the parental attack is highly dependent on the irreverence, disruption, and rebellion of the children. But parents are incapable of any conscious coalition with the children. While it is to their advantage that the children succeed in their rebellion, their educational ideology prevents them from affirming and supporting the rebellion. Then, once a teacher (Peters) is able to communicate with parents (Jackson), the parents suspend their attack on the teachers and join forces with Midway's staff in a war against the children.

Midway's children are perhaps unaware of the significant effect they have on Midway's larger politics. They are aware of the immediate effect they have on their teachers and the damage they are able to inflict on the physical plant of the school; but they are unaware of the significant part they play in the parental attack on the school. Midway's children are able to affect vitally Midway's politics without adult support. Of late, adults with a Black-power ideology have been attempting with some success to organize the children for more disciplined political activity. It remains to be seen whether a more conscious coalition between Midway's children, their "We March Together" organizers, and Midway's parents can be developed as a basis for coordinated political activity.

As limited and unorganized as the unconscious coalition between the parents and the children is, they were, in their separate attacks on the school, able to bring enough pressure to force the exit of Dobson, Ryley, and Morton and to replace them with a Black administration. But the impossible position Dobson found himself in and the passiveness of his character certainly made it easier.

Too well-integrated into the principal's caste and tied to the higher administrative echelons, Dobson was incapable of responding to changing events at Midway. His earlier training did not prepare him for the possibility of ghetto parents becoming a significant reference group that he would have to respond to with the same degree of care and flexibility with which he responded to his superiors. But in the end, his bureaucratic training put him at a disadvantage. He allowed Stratton to make crucial decisions for him and then accepted the responsibility for the decisions when they backfired. Not only was he unable to control his school, but he was unable to transfer responsibility for the lack of control onto his teachers. This was his undoing.

Stratton's replacing the white administration with a Black one can be interpreted as both a shrewd political move and a concession to community pressure. But replacing white with Black or "loose" with "tight" are options of relatively little effect when weighed against the on-going political task that Midway performs for American society.

Midway's central defining characteristic is the discrepancy between its educational ideology of social amelioration and upward mobility and its reality of communicating failure and military control. All of Midway's participants are forced to respond to this central contradiction. That is to say, Midway's internal politics obtain their character from larger political events that do not originate in the school. Since Midway is an instrument of and not the creator of policy, Midway's participants battle with each other over issues in the school. They may be unaware that the terms under which they are forced to fight are terms over which they have no control. Each of Midway's participants, teachers, parents, administrators, and children respond to local events and attempt to maximize their opportunities in the school and minimize defeat. Each participant can assess his situation in relation to these internal events.

Over a period of time battles between parents, teachers, administrators, and children are fought out; victories are won; defeats are suffered; coalitions change; children and teachers are destroyed; parental pressure is now unchecked, now contained; administrations come and go. But with all these confrontations, regroupings, and significant changes in the tone of the school as it appears to its participants, Midway's political task of social control and class placement does not change.

MIDWAY REGARDS itself as an agent of mobility for its children. But American society is unwilling or unable to absorb large numbers of Midway's Black and Puerto Rican youth. The fact that Midway's lower-class children do not learn to read, are branded as failures, and subsequently fail to make it into the middle class is not a result of poor administration, incompetent teachers, or lack of funds for educational materials or specialists. Midway's educational failure is not due to an inability of white middle-class teachers to *relate* to ghetto children. It is not due to a failure to communicate.

Those politicians, educational professionals, university professors, and social critics who are directly aware of Midway would like to blame the school's failure on budgetary insufficiencies, administrative inadequacies, and personnel difficulties. In their various reflections on Midway, they focus on the failure of educational policy rather than the logic of the policy itself. For to see the logical relationship between Midway School, its lower-class youth, and the political reality in American society would complicate the white liberal's idea of his humanity and moral superiority. The middle-class liberal is committed to viewing ghetto education as a failure to implement his liberalism and nothing more. One alternative he fails to consider is that Midway operates in the service not of his morality but of his social and economic interests. He cannot afford to see that, in an important sense, Midway has not failed.

Midway's inability to move its children toward the middle class stems from a larger political reality which transcends the intentions of those politicians, planners, and social critics who stimulate and legislate policy in government and those teachers and administrators who apply policy directly in the school. Midway's educational policy transcends the abstract morality of those suburbanites, professors, professionals, and corporate liberals who lend financial and ideological support to ghetto education. When Midway is seen, not as an instrument of liberal ideology but of political reality, it becomes clear that the school's task is the exact opposite of its publicly stated purpose. In a time when American society is unprepared to absorb its lower-class youth into the middle class, Midway successfully serves the purpose of not training its children for middle-class life.

The children's experience in Midway is one of daily defeat and failure. But the children are not told that they are failing because they are lower-class Blacks and Puerto Ricans. They are not informed that their failure is institutionalized and semiautomatic. They are not advised of the political significance of their failure. They are informed that they are failing because they are not learning to read. For it is crucial to Midway's stability that it appear as if the children are failing because of what they fail to learn.

In extensive contact with agents of white society, Midway's children learn that they are unworthy of entrance into middle-class society. They are told and shown that because of their "stupidity" and "disruptiveness" they are not going to college or toward a decent job. They discover that they are not going anywhere. But their education in Midway is not entirely negative. For while being inculcated with their unsuitability for middle-class life, they *are* being prepared for lower-class life. The nature of their contact with Midway's teachers and administrators prepares them for future relations with welfare bureaucracies, police agencies, and lower-level jobs. Their activity in the counter-world prepares them for underground activity in the ghetto. In effect, Midway School with its white authorities and Black functionaries serving them, its tight control, its lack of opportunities, its atmosphere of failure, and its seething underworld is a microcosm of the ghetto. For the children, Midway is a laboratory in which all the themes, realities, and terms of lower-class ghetto life are learned.

Midway's parents take the failure of their children personally and hold the school and its staff responsible. But in their anxiety about their children's futures and their belief that their children must be controlled if they are to be educated, they join with teachers and administrators in containing the children's rebellion. Midway's Black teachers also resolve their conflict of interest by throwing in their lot with the adult world. Thus a potential war of Black against white is transformed into an actual war of adults against children.

In the midst of this war, the administration attempts to impose its bureaucratic blandness and reasonableness with the hope of evading hostility and mediating the conflicts of parents, teachers, and children. When the mediation fails, the administration offers guidance programs, ameliorative programs, and public relations to dilute and cover up the underlying turmoil and to project a more positive image of Midway's daily life. Ultimately most of these programs fail and the Black teachers and Kerner generation teachers prevent total chaos, fill the administrative gap, and restore some semblance of order. It remains to be seen what effect a formally Black administration will have on the tone of the school.

Midway's teachers are the carriers of political policy on a direct and personal level. They are the human link between American society and Midway's ghetto youth. As American society's representatives in Randolph Park, they transmit the terms of success to Midway's children, communicate the failure when the terms are not met, and repress as best they can youthful rebellion against the terms.

Actually Midway's acute teachers are unprepared for the task assigned them. The abstract morality of their suburban and academic past does not prepare them for ghetto education. Their assumption that teaching will provide an arena for the expression of their humanitarianism is severely tested by their initiation into Midway's life. Destroyed by the children and forced to fall back on the illiberal techniques they so despise, many experience the bankruptcy of their liberalism. Others find a new ideology more compatible with the demands of the task. They join a cadre of seasoned veterans chronically adjusted to classroom warfare in the ghetto.

Irrespective of the suitability of the acute teachers for the task, the degree of competence gained from Midway's on-the-job training program, or the compensations of the counter-world, the job of classroom control and class placement gets done. But like harassed colonial administrators doing the dirty work for the mother country, they must directly face the natives' discontent. Midway's teachers find themselves on the front lines of a vast domestic army supported and financed by American society. In exchange for being exempted from Vietnam, they fight a less bloody but equally important war with victories, defeats, and casualties on both sides. But, given the priority of domestic stability and social control, these casualties are expendable. And like their foreign wars, Americans can watch these domestic battles, from a distance, on TV.

Midway and other ghetto schools offer their viewing audience a wide variety of battles, conflicts, and confrontations, all of which may change the immediate situation of their participants. But changes in the tone of the school, changes in administration, changes in internal politics do not necessarily affect the political task that Midway performs for

American society. The consequences of Midway's internal politics determine only the degree of smoothness with which the task is performed. Like a factory that operates with greater or lesser degrees of efficiency according to the competence of its managers, the discipline of its employees, the amount of stockholder interference, and the degree of control over its product, Midway School, with assembly-line regularity, turns out children trained for life in the ghetto. If Midway's task is to change, the change will probably not result from events that occur within the school but from larger battles, broader realignments, more pervasive changes in American society. At present there is no certain indication if and when these changes will take place, what they will be, and what the future task of Midway might become.

Midway's teachers and administrators would like to see themselves as benefactors of the poor. In fact they are agents of ghetto youth repression. American society would like to think of Midway as an instrument of the American dream. In fact, Midway is an instrument of the organizational control and perpetuation of the lower class. With class politics cloaked 'n the language of liberal education and domestic pacification cloaked in the language of social amelioration, Midway illustrates the contradictions of a society committed to the American dream in a period when that dream is becoming less and less realizable.

POSTSCRIPT:

THE HUMANISTIC TEACHER

There is one teacher at Midway who appears to transcend all of the school's destructive processes. Mrs. Stern, in her relationship with the children, applies none of the manipulative or brutal techniques so characteristic of her colleagues. Control in her second-grade class never seems to become an issue inasmuch as the children are obviously involved with her and the projects that she initiates. At the end of the school day, when she walks the children to the exit and says goodbye to each, kisses and hugs are exchanged.

On the day immediately following the assassination of Martin Luther King, when many of the teachers were joking half seriously about whether or not there would be a riot in the school, I visited Mrs. Stern's class. Soberly she asked each child what he thought about the assassination. What followed was a discussion of race relations that I will never forget. The children talked about King in the most personal terms as a great leader whom they had lost and who could not be replaced. Many broke down and cried. The discussion then shifted to the relationship between Mrs. Stern, as a white teacher, and the children. She expressed her doubt as to whether at this time in history, when the Black people were treated so poorly by the white race, Black and white people could really communicate with each other, trust each other, and love each other. She told the children that she loved each one of them and that she tried to understand them, but that she wondered if she could know how it feels to be a Black child living in Randolph Park. The children replied that they loved her in return but that she couldn't ever really know how they lived.

A history of Mrs. Stern's relationship to children in a school that severely limits the possibility of such relationships could be a study in itself and would be perhaps as important as the description and analysis of Midway offered here. Herbert Kohl, in his book *36 Children,* has rendered such a history. The only point to be made here is that whatever the institutional realities of Midway or any other ghetto school, there is often an extraordinary individual who transcends these institutional realities—who can be a teacher in the best sense of the term and who can remain a human being. But a few extraordinary teachers or principals cannot in any major way affect the larger process of ghetto education. Only major institutional changes in American society that allow for a more equitable treatment of its lower classes can measurably affect the brutal reality of ghetto education.